INTERNATIONAL FOOTBALL BOOK
No.12

'Defenders are the labourers of football' said Derby manager Brian Clough. 'What about a bit of the glamour?' retorts Chelsea's David Webb, in his IFB article: and here he makes his point by winning the ball in spectacular fashion from Derby skipper Dave Mackay.

INTERNATIONAL FOOTBALL BOOK

No. 12

Edited by Stratton Smith
Contributing Editors:
PETER JONES and ERIC BATTY

with contributions by

SIR STANLEY ROUS   SIR MATT BUSBY

DON REVIE   ALLAN CLARKE   FRANCIS LEE

NOBBY STILES   DAVID WEBB   MALCOLM ALLISON

JOE ROYLE   JIMMY GREAVES   COLIN STEIN

HARRY HOOD   GEOFF HURST   BOB McNAB

RON DAVIES   WLODZIMIERZ LUBANSKI

GERD MULLER   PIETRO ANASTASI   SALIF KEITA

OSCAR MAS   GERSON SABIDO   KAROLY SOOS

DON ROGERS   ROGER McGOUGH   GEOFFREY GREEN

BRIAN GLANVILLE   GORDON JEFFERY

DRAGAN DZAJIC

SOUVENIR PRESS LTD . LONDON

First published by Souvenir Press Ltd., London, W.1, and
simultaneously in Canada by The Ryerson Press, Toronto, 2

ISBN 0 285 50282 4

Printed in Great Britain by
Bookprint Limited, Crawley, Sussex

CONTENTS

5

CONTENTS

LIST OF ILLUSTRATIONS

7

'Dual control is going to become inevitable in big clubs' says Sir Matt Busby, seen here with Wilf McGuinness when handing over control of Manchester United's team affairs.

NEW WAYS FOR THE '70s

By Sir Matt Busby

NOW that I have left Manchester United's team affairs in the capable hands of young Wilf McGuinness I have had more time to stand back and examine exactly where football is going.

Soccer in the 'seventies is now with us and as general manager it is even more my responsibility to see that Manchester United share in the future.

Incidentally, the dual control of affairs is a system that will have to come to all the big clubs. There are not enough hours in the day for any one man to coach, train, groom, discover players, discipline them, look

9

after them and still manage all the other affairs of a club which has to become even bigger to compete successfully.

I have spent much of the last 12 months talking with architects and committees discussing the Old Trafford of the '70s. We have even discussed the possibility of putting a roof over Old Trafford to turn it into a vast indoor arena. Right now, at an estimated cost of anything up to £1 million, it probably isn't practical but with the development of new techniques and materials it could well come in the future.

And that incidentally would also mean an artificial playing surface which would end the lottery of mud and ice which has never appealed to me.

We have also discussed different methods of pitch protection. We have investigated our car parking problem, and this could involve the possibility of tunnelling. Certainly on the stocks at Old Trafford is a new stand at our scoreboard end to give us

Once again, a great year for George Best, who has surely become one of football's all-time 'Golden boys'? (Below, right) George shows his chipper-skipper look during a Majorca holiday; (above) the look the world knows and loves, Best's fantastic acceleration as he leaves West Ham's Bobby Howell stranded. (Top, left) leaping Best at his kangaroo best, soaring over the Q.P.R. defence, and below, one of those rewards which come so frequently and deservedly: France's Max Urbini presents Best with the European Footballer of the Year Trophy.

covered seats all the way round the ground, with just narrow paddocks in front.

I see this as being a really decisive blow at the problem of hooliganism, which looks like being the biggest headache for football in this decade.

We believe that fans are less likely to misbehave if they all have a seat. They can be controlled and identified, while the few remaining spectators in the standing paddocks can be more closely supervised.

At Old Trafford, Manchester United spend £10,000 a year for police services and they do a good job for us. We are reasonably proud of our control

Another Best—but this time the Ipswich goalkeeper (left), here ever-so-gracefully pushing for a corner under the challenge of Manchester United's Brian Kidd. (Below) a fine shot of the immortal Denis Law, thundering past Crystal Palace 'keeper Jackson.

inside the ground, though what can be done when so-called supporters run amok on trains and in areas far from the actual grounds, is another matter.

I have always advocated stiffer sentences, though I did stop in my tracks last season when a man at Leeds was jailed for two and a half years. But this man had ten previous convictions for offences at football matches so no one could say he did not have his chance.

At the same time what is the difference between a Soccer hooligan and any other kind of hooligan? I ask that because around the time that this fan was sent to prison we were hearing of hippies and student demonstrators escaping with punishments far less severe.

The police get a lot of abuse from football fans, but their skirmishes with the students were not exactly tea parties. It seems strange that even these kind of people can knock the police about and get away with it. Perhaps being a bit of an intellectual has something to do with it. But at least it makes it clear that hooliganism is not just football's problem and while we in the game must do our best to sort out the difficulties, we should not get too much of a guilt complex. Vandalism and teenage gang warfare is a problem of our times and football must press on regardless, as I am sure it will.

The main thing is what happens out on the field. You could give the fans armchairs and free fags, but without something worth watching they won't come. I don't believe in sighing too much for the good old days. They weren't all that good anyway. The game today is better, faster, and more skilful. Play and the players will go on improving. Alex James would still be great today, but he would have to work harder, run faster and know more.

The quarter of a million transfer is not far away. In fact if West Ham had agreed, we would have willingly gone over £200,000 to sign Geoff Hurst two years ago.

I can see prices for the best seats at the big matches rising to £3 and more, but I think the fans will still get value for money in the exciting '70s ahead.

Bobby Charlton, long-time hero of Manchester United and England, shows a thing or two to West Ham's Lindsay.

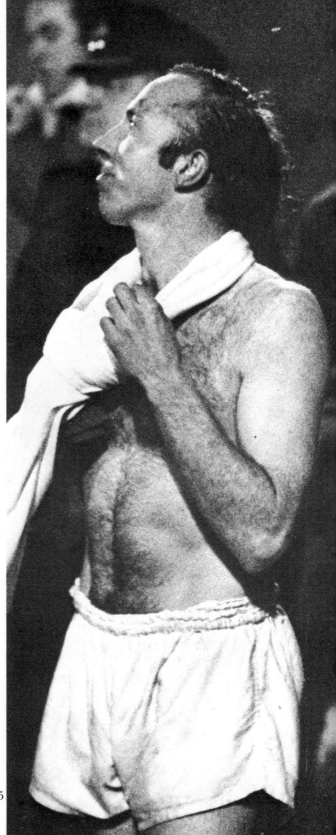

NOBBY STILES

'ENGLAND BALANCED MY PLAY'

By NOBBY STILES

(Manchester United and England)

THERE is no club like Manchester United, but at the same time I must say that my international football has also brought me a great deal of satisfaction.

Occasionally you hear players say they don't care if they never play for England again, and I know there are a few who have gone sour on international football.

Perhaps I have been more fortunate in my experience of this grade of the game because I have no doubts . . . England means a lot to me.

I realised just how much when I was fighting for my fitness last summer and missed the opening of the season. For I also found myself out in the international cold and wondering if I would ever get the opportunity to win a place for the World Cup in Mexico.

The World Cup of 1966 was such a tremendous experience that I was really looking forward to

Game over, the roar of the crowd—Nobby Stiles pauses after a Manchester United victory to savour that very special moment.

15

playing for England as champions. Yet I seemed to miss more internationals than I played after the triumph at Wembley when we beat Germany in that dramatic Final. I was particularly disappointed to miss the important acclimatisation tour of South America in the summer of 1969.

My troubles first started in October, 1967, just a year after the World Cup in England that seemed to transform my career and make me into a footballer of some standing instead of just that 'Niggly little man' from Manchester.

I remember so clearly being carried off in pouring rain against Sheffield United at Bramall Lane after being tackled and falling awkwardly.

It meant a cartilage operation and although I got back into the United team by the end of the season I made only 20 League appearances that year.

Season 1968–69 was better—until that fateful Milan game!

Actually, right through the season my same right knee had been playing up again, suddenly locking in the middle of matches. Usually it eased immediately, but in the European Cup semi-final in Milan in May last year, I had to be carried off and it wasn't until an hour after the game that I could walk properly.

I got through the return leg against the Italians, but an operation had to come to remove the damaged cartilage. It cost me more caps and made me wonder if I would ever play for England again—and this upset me because as I say, international honours have meant a lot to me. Indeed, they transformed my career.

Playing for England gave me my name and also made me as a player. It gave me more confidence and it also gave me the experience to balance my play.

As a youngster I used to be up and down. Then for United I had to play a very defensive role. At the

Jackie Charlton in the thick of it, for England against Holland at Wembley: (above, left) 'keeper Van Beueren punches clear from an attacking Charlton; (below) it's defender Charlton being beaten, for once, by Dutch skipper Eykenbroek. (Inset) the formidable Dutch star, Johan Cruyff. (Right) it's Champagne-on-the-rocks for holidaying Manchester United star George Best.

same time my job for England was further upfield and I think this taught me when to run and when to stay back.

Playing for England made me feel much more sure of myself because at Old Trafford I had had to play second fiddle for a long time. In fact it took me four years to establish myself in the United team after making my début.

Although I felt I was playing well at the time, this kind of background doesn't give you much confidence and the internationals when they came were a great boost.

Then I lost ground. After the 1966 World Cup, I seemed to spend all my time crying off matches and training sessions through injury.

When I came back from Milan to discover I had been included on the tour of South America I was very thrilled. But I was also disappointed because once again I had to stand down.

Now I hope my run of bad luck is over. Things often go in cycles in football. For instance, I had some great years as a youngster playing for England schoolboys and then the youths.

After that came four lean years with nothing until things started to swing my way again and I had four great years with about 25 caps. One thing consoled me. I always knew I would get the chance to prove myself for England again if it was at all possible, because Sir Alf Ramsey is a fair man. England are a great set-up. Even to be in the 22 is great.

Ian Ure, whose signing from Arsenal so strengthened Manchester United's defence, is up forward to support Johnny Aston (right) in this attack on the Nottingham Forest goal.

The best is yet to come

By DON REVIE

Don Revie, the master of Elland Road, shows his 'Football Manager of the Year' Trophy . . .

IT is just about ten years ago since I retired after a playing career with five clubs—Leicester City, Manchester City, Hull City, Sunderland, and Leeds United.

In that decade since I hung up my boots I have seen a lot of changes, not only in my personal fortunes but in the game as a whole. And the one which sticks out most to my mind is the way the application of tactics has become part and parcel of present-day Soccer.

Many former, and invariably talented, players seem to take great pride in the fact that they never had a tactical talk or a pre-match get-together in their entire careers. No-one had to tell them how to play the game, they say, their instinctive ability, sharpened by a leavening of experience, was enough to take them to the top of the tree.

A manager must have had an easy job in those days. All he had to do, apparently, was to pin up the team on the notice board in the dressing room, wish his 11 chosen men 'All the best' and send them out to sort things out for themselves when they got out on to the field.

I have even heard of managers who used to insist that their players did not get a sight of the ball after the weekly practice game, which was usually held on a Tuesday.

They reasoned that if a player was starved of the ball for a few days before a match, he would be all

the keener to get at it on the big day.

Britain had always produced the most determined and naturally talented players in the world and we apparently thought that this state of affairs would persist. And while we stood still with our heads in the sand, full of our own importance, the Continentals and the South Americans got their heads down and worked hard at improving their game, both in skill and tactics.

Long before my time, Billy McCracken, the famous Irish international and Newcastle United full-back, worked out an offside trap which threw opposing forward lines into almost complete confusion.

In those days you had to have three opponents nearer to the goal-line to be onside and the way McCracken and his team-mates at St James's Park worked it, Newcastle's opponents could scarcely step out of their own half without the whistle going.

Then, when the Football Association decided, in 1925, to change the offside law to its present form in the hope that goals—the life-blood of the game— would become more prolific, Herbert Chapman, in the middle of taking Huddersfield Town to three successive First Division titles, thought up the 'stopper' centre-half to put the brake on opposing forwards.

He brought it to perfection later with Arsenal and the great Herbie Roberts and proceeded to carry off the League Championship on three more successive occasions with the Highbury club.

The 'stopper' eventually became the standard pattern for defences all over the world. But while we were satisfied and rested on our laurels, for other countries it was only the beginning.

And it was not until the Hungarians came over to Wembley in 1954 and gave our national side a real trouncing and a complete lesson in tactics that we were finally prised out of our complacency.

The might of Leeds' (left) screws up Sheffield United's defence and brings a good save from 'keeper Alan Hodgkinson; Len Badger, meanwhile, finds himself sandwiched by Billy Bremner and Jackie Charlton. (Right, above) Charlton and Mick Jones pile on the pressure against Hungary's Ferencvaros, and below it's Jones winning the mud-battle, and hauling his way goalwards . . .

Never has the game been so aware of tactics, says Don Revie: Here he joins Sheffield United's John Harris (left) and Barnsley's Johnny Steele in a 'think in' at Leeds University.

Even then, there were men high up in our game who said that it was a fluke. Just 'one of those things' which happen now and again in the best regulated circles. It could not happen again, they said. It was my great fortune that I was not with a club where they harboured such foolish thoughts.

At Manchester City men like our manager Les McDowell and our second-team trainer Fred Tilson, who had scored the two goals which had given the Maine Road club victory over Portsmouth in the 1934 Cup Final, saw that the Hungarians really had something of value in playing Hidegkuti as a withdrawn centre-forward and decided to adopt it in our scheme of things.

That was the start of what Henry Rose, that prince of journalists who lost his life in the tragic Munich disaster, tagged and made world-famous as the 'Revie Plan'.

I got my share of publicity and fame out of it, I must admit. But I must give credit where credit is due and I would be less than honest if I did not say that it really should have been called the 'Tilson Plan' or even the 'Williamson Plan'.

It was Fred who, off his own bat, decided to give it a run in our reserve side, and it was John Williamson, our second-string centre-forward and my biggest pal at Maine Road, who put the idea into practice long before it saw the light of day in First Division football.

It was an immediate success in reserve football. With John peeling off from the forward line and operating in midfield, opposing centre-halves did not seem to know whether they were coming or going. Out of the last 25 Central League games that season, the 'stiffs' lost only one.

Manager McDowell decided that the scheme was

'just the job' for the first team and as soon as we reported for training next season we really got down to brass tacks to incorporate it in our plans.

It took us to two successive Cup Final appearances. But the game I remember best with it in operation was a visit to Ibrox to meet the famous Glasgow Rangers side which was carrying all before it North of the Border.

We 'paralysed' them 4–1 in front of a big crowd, the Scottish Press waxed lyrical, and after the game the Rangers fans shook off their disappointment and sang out the invitation 'Will ye no come back again' at the top of their voices.

It was a memorable night for me and it helped to hammer home the value of tactics. It was a lesson I never forgot and one which I vowed I would put into practice if ever I was lucky enough to get a job as a manager.

I got that chance with Leeds United and, with my hand on my heart, I can honestly say that every 18-year-old professional on the Elland Road staff at the present moment knows a lot more than I did about the tactical side of the game when I finished playing.

British football, which has always thrown up the best instinctive players in the world, now leads in skill and tactics as well. And while much of the improvement is due to the foresight of managers and coaches, a lot of credit must also go to the present generation of players who, since the abolition of the maximum wage, have really got right down to the job

I believe, too, that the ultra-defensive football which managers have had forced onto them in their struggle for survival is now on the way out.

And there are plenty of men who are now turning their backs on all-out defence and looking for policies and plans which will produce not only the results but the kind of entertaining football which the knowledgeable spectator wants to see.

To real Soccer fans all over the country, I want to say that I believe your best days are yet to come. The important thing is that we never again allow ourselves to become complacent. Anyone who thinks he knows the lot is either a fool or a 'nut-case'. And there are not many of those earning a living in this great game of ours these days. Take my word for it.

23

Another—and very typical—shot of that fierce little man, Billy Bremner . . .

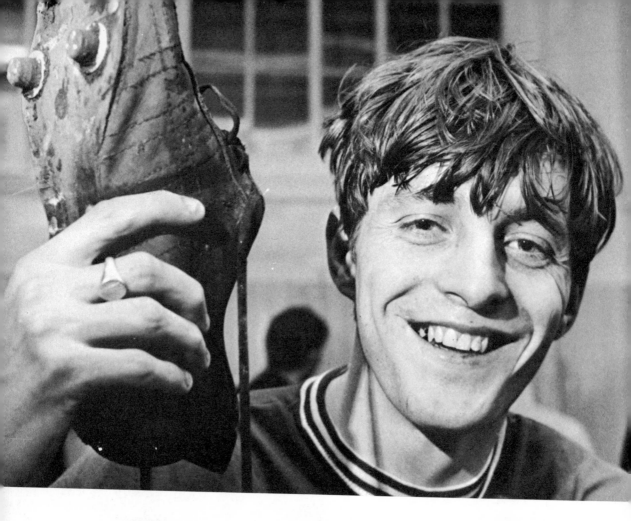

Clarke's could be first million-pound family!

By ALLAN CLARKE
(Leeds United and England)

FULHAM—and England—owe a lot to Johnny Haynes and George Cohen. They have been shining stars for both club and country for many years. Their skill and ability has been admired by football fans the world over.

In my book, too, they are a couple of great fellows

who, unlike many of their contemporaries, turned their backs on opportunities to join bigger and better clubs, to give the 'lot' to the team which gave them the chance of fame and fortune as youngsters.

No club has had better and more loyal servants and I want to put it on record that I will be eternally grateful to them for the help and encouragement they gave to me when, as an 18-year-old I was transferred to Fulham from my home-town team, Walsall.

In my short career in the game I have known other players who had no thoughts but for themselves. George and Johnny were just the opposite and I could not have done better if I had been able to hand-pick my tutors. But I did not even have to ask.

Cohen, then a current England star, took me under his wing from the word 'go'. After the games we played together for the Craven Cottage club before he got the injury which brought a tragic and premature end to a brilliant career, he never failed to take me on one side and, in the nicest possible way, point out where he thought I had gone wrong and what I should do about putting it right.

Even when the accident kept him sitting on the touch-line he made a habit of coming round to my home every Sunday morning and, over a cup of tea, going through the game to point out my strengths and weaknesses. And when I used to get a little argumentative he would point out in his quiet manner that the 'spectator often sees more of the game than the man who is playing'.

No matter how far I go in the game I will never forget George Cohen—player extraordinary and the nicest fellow I have met.

In fact, George's friendship meant so much to me that I was not too keen on joining Leicester City. When I did go the gossips had it that the reason I moved was because Johnny Haynes and I did not see eye to eye. And that is just about the biggest load of nonsense I have heard.

Johnny may have lost some of the speed of thought and movement which made him the mainspring of England's attack for so many years, but he was still the most accurate passer of the ball in the game. It

Goal!—and as Allan Clarke wheels away, delighted, Spurs' Peter Collins slumps in his tracks . . .

25

may have looked as if the whole team had to revolve round Johnny Haynes—or else. But the truth was that he was so good at 'showing' himself in the open space to make himself available for a ball out of defence that he was always a lot easier to find than anyone else.

And when he got it he could still 'make it talk'. Billy Bremner has often told me that Haynes was his idol when he was a schoolboy in Stirling. Even now, when he puts a ball astray he mentally chides himself 'Haynesy would have done better than that!'

I am in complete agreement with Bill. In my career so far I have not enjoyed playing with anyone better. It was an education in itself. Find a couple of yards to 'work' in and Johnny would see that you got service at the vital moment. He was playing his heart out for Fulham and he never had any time for anyone who put self before side.

Those are my sentiments, too, despite the criticism I came in for during my brief stay with Leicester. I know as well as anyone that a professional footballer must play anywhere his manager orders. And the fact that I won the 'player of the match' award in the Cup Final against Manchester City when I was playing in the midfield role manager Frank O'Farrell asked me to adopt, must prove something.

But I am the first to admit that I was not happy doing it. I had always been a 'striker' and it was entirely strange to me. I honestly did not think I was doing justice to the side or myself. And while I admit I said so openly, I certainly tried my best whenever I went onto the field.

Thanks to the teachings of Cohen and Haynes I would not know how to do otherwise. But the value of team spirit had been hammered into me long before I met these two stars.

My father had played as a part-timer with the Welsh club Bangor City while working as a lorry-driver. He was football 'daft' and had five sons, of whom I am the second. When birthdays or Christmas came around nobody had to think what presents to give us.

It was always a pair of football boots or a strip in the colours of the Midlands team which was doing best at that moment. And every spare minute was spent learning the game on the playing fields right opposite the house where we were all born.

Already, three of us have signed as professionals with League clubs. Frank, the eldest, has seen service at Shrewsbury and Queens Park Rangers. I nearly signed for Aston Villa, but Walsall, Fulham, Leicester and Leeds United have been the clubs in my career so far. And that, I hope is how it will end.

Number three son Kevin, is now with Wolves after starting at Walsall. And even at 17 the Molineux club thought him good enough to risk a £20,000 fee.

Like my dad we are all 'strikers' and there are two more yet to come in—12-year-old Kelvin, who is already looking the part with South Staffordshire Schoolboys, and eight-year-old Wayne.

It is Father's ambition to have us all playing in League football at the same time. And as Frank is only just 28 there's a good chance that he could see his dream come true.

Ever since we were 'nippers' he has seen that we all

The stuff that £165,000 is made of—Allan Clarke beats Wednesday's wing-half Gerry Young and slips home a winner at Hillsborough.

*'Hey! What's it all about, then?'—Manchester City 'keeper Mulhern is grounded, and virtually caged by
Jackie Charlton's big legs; but Booth has that ball coolly under control.*

worked towards his ambition by helping the junior members of our family with advice and encouragement.

It was Frank who spent hours making me kick with my left foot which was a real 'swinger' in my schooldays. In my turn I had to pass on the benefit of my experience to Derek—the only natural left-footed player in the family—who, in turn, is now concentrating on Kelvin.

'One for all and all for one' is the Clarke family motto and if we ever manage to achieve my father's ambition and transfer fees keep on in their rising spiral, it is on the cards that the 'Frank Clarke Five'

could be the first £1,000,000 family in the history of Football.

That would be 'the end' as far as Clarke senior is concerned and, from the five of us, it would be a wonderful way of showing Mother how much we all appreciate all the hard work she has put in washing thousands of football strips over the years so that her sons would be the smartest members of their teams.

She may not know a lot about football but she has always told us 'if you look the part, you are a long way to success'. With advice like that and all the help I have received from men like Cohen and Haynes, I just had to prove myself.

ENGLISH F.A. SHOULD BAN REGISTRATION OF SCOTS

—a help for the game in the north

By MALCOLM ALLISON
(Manchester City assistant manager and coach)

WHAT'S gone wrong with Scottish football? The Scots failed to qualify for the World Cup in England in 1966 and they put up a poor show trying to reach Mexico this year. In fact I think it is high time Scotland put their house in order and took a long, hard look at the state of their game north of the border.

In my view the fans up there are getting a raw deal. Scotland is a country rich in football talent. They have produced immortal players in the past and they are still doing so. Outstanding Scots are sprinkled throughout English football, and they have good players in their own League.

Yet at neither international nor club level have Scotland ever really achieved anything.

I suppose Celtic's European Cup win is one piece of evidence to the contrary, but it was an isolated event and they also had the good fortune to meet Inter Milan in the final, a team who were coming down on a slide.

In international terms it was a disgrace that they failed to qualify for the World Cup and Scotland should be asking themselves why they have so consistently failed to make the impact their native talent deserves.

I believe Scotland should seriously consider ways and means of stopping their players emigrating to the game in England. This incidentally goes for the Irish as well. I think it is wrong that this country should milk the cream of their players and ap-

parently get away with it for so long.

You can't blame the players of course, because everyone has the right to better himself if he can. The responsibility rests with the Scottish FA who should be striving to keep their top men at home.

It might be difficult to do it from the Scottish end, but have they ever really thought of getting the English Football Association to forbid the registration of Scottish players . . . as they already do to the European countries?

It is also wrong that clubs here should be allowed to take boys from school in Scotland. The authorities did make a half-hearted gesture in preventing Scottish schoolboy stars being taken on by English clubs as apprentice professionals.

But they haven't really stopped the drift. The boys still come, only as amateurs ostensibly coming here to take jobs outside football.

Of course English football would be the losers. We wouldn't have had those colourful Scottish characters like Denis Law, Dave Mackay, Billy Bremner, Jim Baxter and Pat Crerand.

But I am looking at things from the Scottish point of view and those same players would have been helping to pull in the fans up North, making Scottish football prosperous and healthy.

As it is, it seems to me that Scotland is complacent and happy to accept the big fees—outrageous fees at times—that English clubs pay for their players to help keep their game going.

This is negative. They would do much better building their own sides, attracting their own crowds and making their own money.

It's time the Scottish FA got their heads out of the sand. They have always lagged behind the English FA, and you can hardly say that our leaders are trendy pace-setters!

Their coaching courses are inferior to those here and I understand they have only recently introduced the idea of associated schoolboys, which is a system operating here for some time now.

Meanwhile Scotland struggles on and their immediate problem is how to improve their flagging international standard. There has always been the controversy over whether they should call up their Anglo-Scots for internationals and I have come round to the opinion that they would be better off

Malcolm Allison—'Why bother to pick the Anglos?'

without them.

They would do better concentrating on their own players, even if they are inferior, because the Scottish FA could get things organised like the English FA and order clubs to release players.

But I must stress that this is only a short-term policy. The real answer is to keep the star Scots at home, and then we really would see a top Soccer nation, and not as at present, a second-class bunch of also-rans.

Whatever has happened to Scotland's might? asks Malcolm Allison. The goal that put Celtic out of the European Cup, scored by Milan's Piero Prati at Parkhead

By FRANCIS LEE

(Manchester City and England)

MALCOLM ALLISON shouted 'Attention!' and Manchester City's men promptly leapt to their feet and our first refereeing teach-in was under way.

'Stand easy', said Malcolm, and we all relaxed as Mr Dave Wallace began to run through the points raised in the Football League circular sent to all clubs last season.

Mr Wallace asked if we had all read the circular and, of course, he was asked what circular—we hadn't had one! Not being a bad judge, the referee

ignored that sally, but it wasn't the end of the ribbing.

In fact, we hadn't had such a hilarious preparation for a match for a long time, though let me assure you that we weren't trying to take the micky out of the referee or anything like that.

It's just that our dressing-room seems to be a breeding ground for wags and we didn't see any cause to make an exception for the referee. In fact, I believe we helped him in the long run because we relaxed the atmosphere, and if he was a shy man we

30

England against Wales at Wembley—and it's Francis Lee scoring a fine winner . . .

'Referees should spend six-week periods with clubs now and again'

made it much easier for him to put his message across.

But he wasn't giving anything away and he looked more like a poker player with three aces and a couple of kings than a referee as he kept a deadpan face during the proceedings.

He forced a slight smile when he stressed that everyone must be ten yards from the ball when a free kick was taken and Malcolm asked him if this would apply to the other side as well.

By this time he had twigged that our dressing room is a little bit like a pub tap-room, complete with the variety acts.

We always try for a bit of a song. For instance, if Colin Bell is having a bit of special treatment, we always give him a chorus or two of, 'We'll drink a drink a drink to Colin the king . . .'

No one gets away with anything, like when Mike Doyle had a particularly good write-up in the papers, we sang about 'Magnificent Mike in his Number four shirt'.

Last season's visit by referees to explain controversial points in the dressing rooms all over the country was a special occasion. In addition to the referee we had another visitor to our dressing-room, Ernie Marples, the Tory ex-Transport Minister.

When he came in he got a rousing reception with 'For He's a Jolly Good Fellow'.

He had a ball with him which he wanted us to autograph for charity. We asked him if it was for Harold Wilson's testimonial! Anyway, we duly signed, and after congratulating him on the motorways we asked him if he would support income-tax exemption for professional footballers.

But aside from the joking—and the referee had the last laugh with a penalty against us—I thought the referee's visit a sound idea. Anything to bring closer understanding between players and officials must help the game.

I would like to see the idea taken further and I suggest referees, if they can get away from their jobs, should spend six-week periods with clubs every now

and again.

Perhaps they could spend part of their holidays allocated to a club. I would like them to see our training and listen to what our coaches are telling us and demanding of us.

I suppose a referee officiates at about 40 games a season and the rest of the time is theory. But if he joined a club for a short period he could really get a close up of what goes on. He could take charge of practice matches and he would be able to pick up a side of the game he never sees and which I think he should see.

At the same time I don't believe in referees getting too chummy with players. I have thought for a long time that they should be treated more like judges, detached and anonymous.

For instance, I don't like the trend in the game which is giving referees more publicity. You often see their career and hobbies described in club programmes. I don't think their names should even be published in the programmes.

If referees were given the same kind of standing as judges then perhaps players would accept their authority a little more respectfully.

Gary Sprake is down, and safely on the ball—meanwhile Rodrigues shields him from England's driving Lee . . . (Right) Derby's Les Green comes off best after a corner-kick, but Dave Mackay doesn't look too happy about Colin Bell's broad back being so very, very close . . .

'Juanito'—mascot of the 1970 World Cup.

By GEOFF HURST

(West Ham and England)

If only the Argentinians had stuck to football...

IF IT'S true that one match can be the making of a player, then I suppose everyone would nominate the 1966 World Cup Final at Wembley as the match that made me. Well, maybe that game did do a lot for me—in more ways than one—but I reckon the quarter-final with Argentina was the most significant match for me in that memorable series.

It's been described as the most incredible 90 minutes ever seen on a football pitch. It would be hard to argue with that. But first, why was it so important for me? That's easy. I would never have played in it but for the fact that Jimmy Greaves was injured in the previous game against France.

After a pretty disappointing pre-World Cup tour of Scandinavia I didn't fancy my chances of getting back into the England team, let alone displacing England's top goal-scorer. But that unfortunate injury to Jimmy gave me the chance I had been waiting for, and a second bite at the cherry.

Getting back to the Argentinians—I think they may have beaten us if they had stuck to playing football. They had two great forwards in Onega and Mas and a superb half-back in Marzolini who proved to be one of the most outstanding defenders in the 1966 competition.

Geoff Hurst—the man Matt Busby tried to make the 'first quarter-million-pound signing'. Hurst says, 'It's sheer hard work, that's all'—and here he is, putting it in against Nottingham Forest . . .

But, as you have no doubt read, football took a back seat to kicking, tripping, and holding, and the expected Soccer spectacular was turned into a shambles. One moment however in that game stands out for me . . . the moment when I scored England's winning goal to guarantee my place in the latter stages.

It came in the 77th minute. Martin Peters, my West Ham team-mate, floated the ball over from the left deep into the Argentine defence. It was the chance I'd been waiting for. I ran in to meet the ball at just the right moment and managed to head it past Roma the Argentine goalkeeper before their defence sensed the danger.

Then came the epic semi-final with Portugal, and after it those three goals in the Final against West Germany. Of course, that historic hat-trick in the Final will rank as the most memorable performance in my career, but I still regard the goal against Argentina as the most *important* of my career.

Scoring goals, of course, is what I get paid for. And, believe me, they get harder every season. Strikers, by the very nature of their role in modern football, are the most shadowed men in the game and get the 'full star treatment' every time they walk on the pitch, whether it is at club or inter-national level.

This means you come in for a fair bit of 'stick' on the pitch, and believe me I've got the bumps and bruises to prove it. Often, in club matches, I find that two men are detailed to tag me. So you can't afford to stand still. Often the only way to make space for yourself is to try a couple of dummy runs so that when the ball is played to you, you have the luxury of a few feet to work in.

I think that over the last five seasons I have managed to maintain scoring consistency. To attain this, you have to set yourself high standards. I usually aim for around 30 goals a season. If I fall short of the mark I reckon I haven't had a successful season.

Mind you, setting targets of achievement can be a frightening thing in football today, where goals are

Martin Peters, Hurst's brilliant West Ham team-mate (left) wins this one in the air from Liverpool's Ian St. John. (Right) one of the snappiest Soccer pix of the year— Chelsea's Tommy Baldwin making a despairing lunge at West Ham's Eddie Bovington. . . .

being shared around. But I honestly believe that it is the only way to keep up a high standard of consistency.

You see I haven't been endowed with the instinctive skills of players like Jimmy Greaves and Bobby Charlton.

Any success I may have had as a striker in football has only come through sheer hard work. Call it dedication if you like. But then I've been lucky to have been brought up in a Soccer Academy like West Ham where I was groomed by players like Malcolm Allison, Noel Cantwell, and Frank O'Farrell—three of today's most successful coach-managers.

Perhaps, again, I was lucky to join a club like West Ham where skills and flair are instilled into a player right from the start. We believe in trying to play positive football. We hate being negative. Dull, defensive football may be alright when you're winning—there may be even some justification for it's retention, if the right results are coming.

But personally I would hate to play for a club that was purely defensively minded. How can you maintain standards by being negative? And standards are something that I prefer to live by. Just remember, any team can destroy; but only the best can create. It is the creators who build for the future, not the destroyers. They only serve to drive the crowds away. And that can't be a good thing for football, can it?

Wife said: 'Oh, blimey! —He's been sent off'

By DAVID WEBB

(Chelsea)

SOMETIMES I feel like getting up on a platform, thumping my fists about in true politician's style and yelling: 'How about a bit more fair play for defenders?' Because, let's be honest, the main glamour of modern Soccer is all there for the attacker—the bloke who bangs in the goals or the mid-field link with the body-swerve and the Gene Kelly-type magic feet.

How come I get so het up about this? Well, for a start I am a defender. There is about 13 stone of me and about six feet of me so I suppose it's only natural that I should be there in the back four.

Fair enough. But it gets a bit niggling when one reads how Brian Clough, for instance, describes the forwards as the 'artists' of the game and the defenders as the 'labourers'.

I don't mind being described as a 'labourer', because I'm a Cockney who has never minded a hard day's work, but I still think the old myth about it being the forwards who have all the artistry should be killed off. Players like Ray Wilson, in his England days, George Cohen, Eddie McCreadie (a Chelsea mate, and a real mate of mine), Terry Cooper of Leeds, and dozens more are technically defenders,

(Above, left) a superb action shot of Chelsea dynamo Alan Birchenall attempting to head a goal against Crystal Palace 'keeper Jackson. (Below) rangy Peter Osgood forces his way through a stranded Everton defence.

but nobody in their right mind could deny that they are also artists.

I suppose it is that old images stay on in Soccer. There are thousands of fans who remember the old picture of a full-back—crew-cut hair style, massive great thighs and shin-pads, characters who looked like barn-doors rather than athletes. They used to prowl around after their opponent, rarely moving up field to join an attack—and more often than not their clearances were about as constructive as a bulldozer demolishing a brick wall.

But times change. We had the over-lapping full-backs—chaps with tremendous speed, ball control and, often, a darned hot shot that wouldn't have disgraced those 'artistic' forwards. Centre-halves like Jackie Charlton going up for corners or up-field free-kicks, leaping and soaring . . . and scoring goals.

Most fans are aware of the changes. They know

about the new role of defenders like myself. But the glamour-tag still sticks with the George Bests, the Francis Lees and the others. 'Fair play for defenders': that's what I want to get across.

Don't mind me talking out like this. It's only human nature where we Cockneys are concerned. My own history in the game is pretty straightforward. I was with West Ham Schools, went along to West Ham while Dave Sexton was there. Went to Orient, while Dave Sexton was there. Then to Southampton where I did okay but missed the essential atmosphere of London . . . and eventually joined Chelsea, where Dave Sexton was manager.

Dave Sexton is a great manager. He's achieved so much at Chelsea, transforming this famous West London side into a consistent fighting machine. No longer do fans the world over take the micky out of Chelsea. No longer does anybody even think of referring to the club as 'The Pensioners'.

Tommy Docherty had started the build-up, then Dave Sexton stepped in. In no time at all, famous managers like Harry Catterick of Everton and Don Revie of Leeds United were saying that Chelsea had the best strength in depth of any First Division club.

And it is the fluidity of style that does the trick. In other words, the 'glamour' is shared round. I suppose every footballer feels a bit envious about the other man's abilities.

Chelsea's brilliant Scottish international Charlie Cooke, with all his dazzling control and ability to pin-point a pass, looks enviously at the chaps who bang in the goals. Some of the hustle-bustle merchants eye Charlie's fantastic skills with envy. I perhaps envy both, but these days the defender can get all the chances he wants to get in among the goals . . .

One Boxing Day not so long ago I got a hat-trick at Ipswich—but I was wearing the number five jersey. Actually this trio of goals, two with my nut and one with my right foot, caused some chaos with my wife Jackie at home. In a news bulletin, they flashed my picture on the screen. 'Oh blimey!' thought Jackie, 'he's been sent off.'

The grace of Charlie Cook—perfectly balanced, the Chelsea forward glides past Everton's Sandy Brown. (Right) not one, but five Peter Bonetti's—five separate exposures of characteristic movements taken at night using exposures of 1/500th of a second at f8 with two synchronised flashes . . . one for the camera buffs.

Actually that hat-trick gave the statisticians something to think about. At first, it was believed that I was the first centre-half to nick three goals in a League game. Then they found that Dickie Rooks, of Middlesbrough, managed the same feat in 1966.

Look through the score-sheets after any Saturday afternoon. You'll see plenty of defender names among the scorers. Full-backs whanging 'em in after a flying touch-line run. Wing-halves coming through from behind and letting fly. But with very few exceptions, the glamour is with the 'orthodox' forwards. They are the boys who pull in the £100,000 transfer fees. They are the ones who decorate the pin-up magazines.

And despite all the new evidence, the defender, specially those numbered two, three and five, are regarded as the good old work-horses, the labourers of the industry.

Anyway, occasionally something happens which makes me feel that the lot of a defender is gradually on the up and up. The season I joined Chelsea (incidentally my first game in the first team was a 3–1 win against Manchester United at Old Trafford and that bucked me up no end), Charlie Cooke was voted Player of the Year by the supporters' club. Pretty predictable, thought I—Charlie's skills were bound to catch the eye.

Then, out of the blue, came the news the following season that the award had gone to me. The odd goals, including that hat-trick, maybe swung the decision but it was highly chuffing for a hardened old number two-or-five like me!

No, I may not be full of the Cooke or Peter Osgood-type skills, but I certainly have a lot of enthusiasm. This helps me get through—and anyway I am never happy unless I'm seeing a lot of the ball.

A 'labourer' I may be, but an enthusiastic one. I just hate being unsuccessful. That's why I'm so keen to help Chelsea really get up there with the giants—in Europe as well as in Britain. One League cham-

A more familiar Bonetti—diving over Chelsea full-back Eddie McCreadie with Wolves' leader Derek Dougan in close and formidable attendance . . .

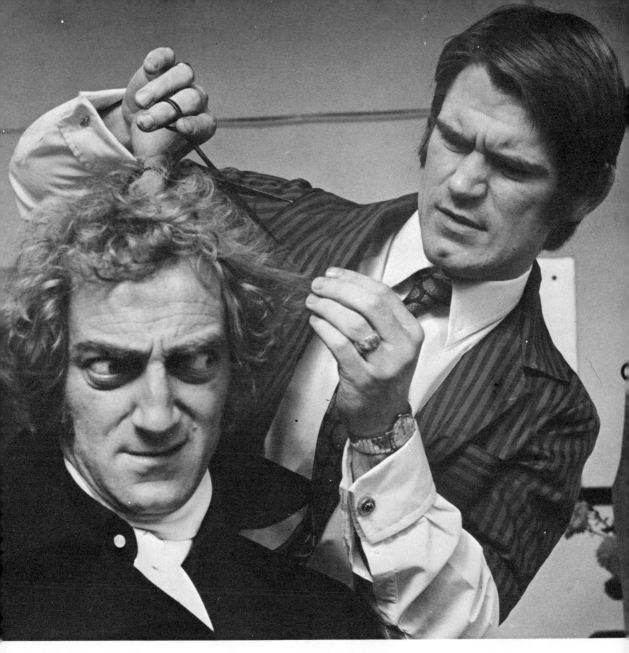

'Who's this fellah think he is, Georgie Best?'—Dave Webb looks a bit dubious about doing his 'Sweeney Todd' on comedian Marty Feldman's mop . . .

pionship and nothing at all in the FA Cup; the record when I got to Stamford Bridge, just wasn't right for such a great club.

Soccer invigorates me. Business excites me. I hate losing at either.

At any rate, two of my personal ambitions are being solved. Surely nobody would dare, right now, to regard Chelsea as a 'joke' side. And slowly but surely defenders are getting a bit more of the spotlight.

So maybe I won't have to form my 'Fair Play for Defenders' party after all!

STOP THE PASS: IT'S EASIER THAN STOPPING THE STARS

By BOB McNAB

(Arsenal and England)

THEY say nothing succeeds like success. That's particularly true of football. Take England's World Cup success in 1966. It revolutionised the game in this country and now nearly every team in the Football League plays to a 4–3–3 or 4–2–4 system.

An Arsenal goof!—(top left) 'keeper Barnett has the ball taken out of his hands by the boot of team-mate George Graham; (below) Terry Neill loses the ball to Everton full-back Wright; (this page, top) Bob McNab sits one out with new signing Peter Marinello from Hibs.

Yet when I first started at Huddersfield as an 18-year-old amateur it used to be the old 'W' formation where full-backs had to cover the centre-half, which left the wingers space. This meant that the wingers were often left loose and had time to pick up speed before they reached you.

In those days there was a set routine for full-backs and forwards. We used to practice long clearances down the touchline to find our centre-forward and put us on the attack.

Today of course all that has changed. If your side has the ball you are attacking; if the other side has it, you are defending. So full-backs have taken on a more creative role. They must be quick to anticipate; quick to exploit an opportunity to attack when it presents itself.

Under the 4–3–3 system we operate at Arsenal two centre-backs cover the middle, acting as control towers of the defence, so that the full-backs can mark the wingers very tight.

Soccer is now a game of zones, and a full-back's duty is to make sure that nobody gets through in his particular zone. The Italians use the man-for-man systems.

If you have to mark a really dangerous winger like George Best or Peter Thompson you must play it really tight and try to ensure that they are so well covered that another opposition forward will think twice about trying to 'find' him, because he is not spare.

Marking players of this calibre of course is an absolutely full-time job. You have to try and stop the ball getting to them in the first place. Believe me, if players of the ability of Best and Thompson get the ball under control first it's very hard to dispossess them.

So anticipation is a vital factor and can save you from committing yourself to an unnecessary tackle. An opponent will often try to lure you away from the touchline to make room for another player to come through for the overlap. So you must always be prepared to counter this tactic.

(Left) Marinello in action for Arsenal against Chelsea— and finding it tough going under the combined defence of McCreadie and Webb; (right) McNab shows his paces and almost leapfrogs Crystal Palace forward Bartram . . .

Players like Geoff Hurst who go out to the wings to find space often try dummy runs and checking to try to 'run you off' the ball. Hurst is a master at checking and going forward to make space for himself. He spins and weaves to set up space for himself and needs very close watching.

Geoff is famed for his near-post headers. But they are the result of split-second timed runs. He just doesn't hang around the area. Often he will go to the far post to create space at the near post so that he can time his run to exploit the gap when the ball is centred.

Like most full-backs these days, I love to attack when the opportunity presents itself. But you can find yourself taking chances—particularly at home—and you may over-commit yourself. If the move breaks down and the other side mount a swift counter-attack it can often cost you a goal.

It's no use making spectacular runs upfield if the man you are marking is left loose to receive the ball and create danger at your own end. A good full back should be judged firstly on his defensive qualities and then on his ability to use the ball in certain attacking situations.

When it comes to attacking full-backs, then my England team-mate Terry Cooper springs immediately to mind. He is far and away the best at 'going forward', which probably stems from his previous experience as a winger with Leeds. But Terry is always conscious of his defensive duties.

Playing in the First Division has helped my game tremendously and I'll never regret moving from Huddersfield to Arsenal although I must admit I really struggled in my first season. After a spell of injuries and loss of form.

I was also dogged by injury at the start of my second season and was in and out of the team like a yo-yo. When I did get back it was always at right-back. But eventually I got my chance at left-back and gradually my confidence came back after I was beginning to be tagged as a jinx man at Highbury.

Everything suddenly went right for me last season and after winning four England caps I went on the South American tour, playing in the FA XI that beat Mexico 4–0.

Now like most England players I'm keeping my fingers crossed. At 26 I'm hoping that the best days for Bob McNab and Arsenal are still in the future.

George Graham supporting Arsenal's 'keeper Wilson makes a great skyline shot at Highbury . . .

Why do we have to feel inferior to England

By RON DAVIES

(Southampton and Wales)

ENGLAND alone were in Mexico to represent the British Isles in the World Cup Finals leaving Wales, Scotland, and Ireland at home, and envying. But one can't help but think that if the other three countries had been afforded the advantages and facilities that were made available to England then they, too, could have been in Mexico taking on the world's best.

Without trying to detract in any way from England's success, I feel the other countries should

Ron Davies up against Manchester United's David Sadler, but it's 'keeper Jimmy Rimmer who gets to the ball first . . .

be treated on the same level; don't allow them to feel inferior to England, as has so often been the case in the past.

While the England manager, Sir Alf Ramsey, is given every assistance by the clubs with regard to pre-match get-togethers and the like, the other three national managers have to wait in hope that the players they have selected will turn up, not two days before as is the case with England, but very often just a couple of hours before the match is due to start. This is where the system slips up. I'm certain that all four Home Countries would have qualified for the World Cup if they had been able to make the same preparations as England.

Wales proved during the Home International Championships last season that when the players are together for a week or more, they are capable of producing a very high standard of football and teamwork. To me, as a man on the inside, it was fascinating to see the difference in spirit among the players during that week, compared to the usual despondency before other internationals. Despite serious injuries which, for one match, robbed us of our entire defence, Wales played some magnificent football during that week.

Against England at Wembley, when we were without Terry Hennessey and Mike England, Wales put on one of their best-ever performances to lead England by 1-0 at half-time. Certainly this was the best Welsh side I had ever played in and, although, we finally lost the game 2-1, we were by no means disgraced. In that first half, we had England all at sea and would have been a match for any side in the world.

Wales and Ireland, more than the other two countries, feel a desperate need for more co-operaion from the clubs. To illustrate this point, look at the England squad. There are so many good players to choose from that one, two or even three injuries are not really missed. And the manager can afford to experiment with his side, as happened in the international against Holland at Wembley when SIX goalscorers lined up in the England side.

Scotland may have a different problem. Certainly with the talent they have available, it seems very strange they aren't a world force in football. But Wales and Ireland have their regular squads and upon them they are entirely dependent. If a man is desperately out of form, the chances are that he will still be selected, simply because there is no one to take his place. When a man is injured and can't play, inexperienced players are often drafted into the side—players who can't command a regular first-team place with their club, or who are not yet old enough to do so.

On a personal level, I find it extremely difficult to play for Wales. The same applies to the Newcastle player, Wyn Davies. We are both used to playing with wingers for our clubs because, as we are both strong in the air, this is a natural weapon for the side we are playing in. Wales play without wingers which means there is a lack of crosses for Wyn and myself to convert into goal chances and also that we have to play a different role to the one we are used to, which, to say the least, is difficult.

If we had a few days together before the game, patterns of play could be worked out that would be to the advantage of each man's capabilities and, ultimately, to the team performance. A team can have the eleven greatest players in the world, but if they are not welded into a team, they'll win nothing.

In the World Cup, Wales were in the same qualifying group as Italy and East Germany. Because of injury, I was able to play in only two of the four games and the Welsh manager, Dave Bowen, was unable to field the same side in any of the matches. In fact, since he took over as the Welsh team manager, Dave has been able to field the team he originally selected on only two occasions—that's out of 31 matches!

Newcastle's Wyn Davies looking for a goal, but Southampton's wing-half Fisher gets the ball clear.

'YOU'RE JUST A PLAY-ACTOR'

—or how a record can follow you around...

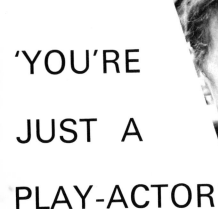

By COLIN STEIN

(Rangers and Scotland)

I HAVE a lot of sympathy for players who get caught up in the fashionable new Hundred Thousand Pounds' Club.

It might not be so difficult to carry the big price tag if it weren't for those who go out of their way to make sure you don't find it easy.

When I went to Rangers from Hibs for the first six-figure transfer in Scotland, I expected and certainly ran into that kind of trouble. I don't object so long as it's fair and square. But it isn't always.

However, I suppose it's the price of fame!

Much as I loved being a Hibs' player, it is fame when you become a Rangers' first-team player. I've heard former Ibrox men like Jock Shaw saying, 'To have worn the light blue gives you a prestige you won't find anywhere else.'

And it's true. From the moment you enter the magnificent Ibrox Stadium and climb the marble staircase, you realise you are in another Soccer world. If nothing else were to happen to me for the rest of my football life, I'd still have the tremendous satisfaction that I had played for the famous Glasgow Rangers.

My paramount ambition, of course, is to be a *great* Ranger. I know tradition is scoffed at in many quarters nowadays as being out of date. We are continually hearing that the past is past—and that we live for the future.

I agree, in part. But no one can ever play for Rangers without being caught up in the great traditions of the club. Players come and go, but if you've been a first-team man of any repute at Ibrox you're remembered for years.

We are constantly confronted by great Rangers of the past . . . George Young, Willie Woodburn, Torry Gillick, Willie Thornton, Ian McColl, Jimmy Millar. The fans never forget those memory-triggering names.

Fame apart, one of the things I've realised most since becoming a Ranger is the necessity for self-discipline which for me is a most difficult task, although I want to stress that I am not a dirty player.

I'm enthusiastic. I fight for every ball. Whether I'm playing for Rangers or Scotland, I want to win. But I repeat, I am not a dirty player.

After being ordered off against Clyde last year,

'The fans expect you always to be scoring goals . . .'—
Here it's a near thing for Colin Stein, playing for Scotland,
as West German 'keeper Maier punches away for a corner.

Stein foiled again . . . this time by St Mirren 'keeper Jim Thorburn, aided by centre-half Ian Young.

however, I realised I could be in a lot of trouble. I'm not saying I was a marked man. But you know the old story! Give a dog a bad name and it sticks. Well a lot of people tried to make the bad name stick to me.

This hurt because as a junior with Armadale, no referee ever had reason to speak to me—never mind order me off.

But as I say, the ordering-off against Clyde was the red light to me, even though it seemed to be fairly generally agreed that I had been under considerable provocation. In the 48 hours that followed the incident, indeed, I had nearly 200 letters from fans sympathising with me.

Even a Celtic fan wrote to tell me he'd seen what happened on TV and while he didn't particularly

fancy me—because of the club I played for, of course —he had to admit I'd been sorely provoked!

I treasure that letter. It's the kindest thing a Celtic man has ever said about me.

It's all right for the armchair critics to say smugly, 'You musn't retaliate.' But it's not easy. Football's a game in which you act and react on the split second. Any player sent off for retaliation has my sympathy. You do things when provoked you wouldn't do in normal circumstances.

After the Clyde ordering-off, however, I resolved to try never to lose my temper; and didn't retaliate the next time a defender was kicking me up and down the field. I kept telling myself the referee would spot it and give me protection. But it kept happening right into the second-half.

Willie Henderson of Rangers cannons a shot off the chest of Celtic's Tommy Gemmell . . . it ran for a corner and Gemmell, we guess, needed quite a chest-rub after the game...

Then I ran into one of the opposition and a foul was given against me. As I ran upfield the ref chased after me and said—'Any more of that and you'll go inside.'

'Referee,' I pleaded, 'I've been kicked up and down this field for almost an hour. Don't I get any protection at all?' His reply knocked me for six. 'You're nothing but a play-actor,' he said. 'Get on with the game!'

He was wrong. I'm not, never have been, a Soccer play-actor. He was also unfair. The foul he'd given me was the first against me in the game.

Despite my determination to keep out of trouble, I was sent off in Toronto against Spurs by World Cup referee Arturo Yamasaki in a close-season friendly. But my so-called crime on that occasion was trifling. I was ruled to have lifted my boot too high in challenging Spurs' 'keeper Pat Jennings.

And not only did Pat speak up for me after the game, so too did Spurs' boss Bill Nicholson who told the Canadian officials—'That was most undeserved —he never even came near the 'keeper.'

Jennings agreed. 'Colin was at least two yards away from me and never made contact' he said. But the incident I think makes my point that if you have a record it follows you around.

One other thing I've found about being a £100,000 striker is that the fans, who are normally encouraging and helpful, always expect you to be scoring goals.

A midfield man or a full-back can get over bad times because his errors aren't always noticed. But if you're supposed to be scoring goals and you're not . . . Heaven help you!

Our manager, I'm glad to say, is always understanding and considerate—even when this striker isn't striking. Finally, let me just say that despite the £100,000 problems it's great to be a Ranger.

At last, for Stein . . . one that didn't get away. He rams a sensational shot past helpless Bilbao 'keeper Angel Iribar three minutes from time at Ibrox . . .

A SPELL IN ENGLAND IS GOOD EXPERIENCE

By HARRY HOOD

(Celtic and Scotland)

FEW players get a second chance to join Celtic. But I am one of the select band; and let me say right away that it is wonderful to be playing for the club I've supported since I was a kid at school.

I'll never know why I turned down the chance to go to Celtic several years ago. Maybe it was sprung on me so quickly that I was in a daze when I was asked to sign.

Celtic and Clyde had reached agreement about a transfer fee. I was called in to complete the deal but because of a few snags I didn't sign. Celtic got impatient and I lost the chance to join them.

Instead I went to Sunderland for a fee of £25,000 —and although I felt I was playing well enough to be a regular member of the first team at Roker Park, manager Ian McColl, who later took over control, obviously didn't. So I returned to Clyde—and Celtic!

I feel, however, that my spell in England has stood me in good stead. My experience has been widened. But not only that. Despite some other opinions, I didn't consider I was a failure down south and believed I was a better player when Clyde bought me back for £11,000.

Many people, I suppose, concluded I hadn't made much of it in England—having gone away for £25,000 and returned less than two years later for less than half that sum. But when I came back to Shawfield I reckon I soon did enough to banish any suggestion that I was a football flop.

Any slight inferiority complex I might have had about coming back at half price—and it IS worrying to be so drastically downgraded—was dispelled when I learned Celtic were interested.

My name was linked with them for about six months before I signed. But all I knew about their interest was from what I read in the newspapers. Nobody said anything to me about it.

Then as the weeks and the months wore on and there was no move, I thought Celtic had forgotten about me. So when they eventually did agree with Clyde on a fee, I jumped at the second chance.

It was always my ambition to play for Celtic. As I said, I've been a fan since my school days. Yet I turned them down, the first time! And now I wonder how this may have changed my career.

Looking back on it, there's no doubt in my mind that my spell with Sunderland was two years in the

Soccer wilderness. I got on well with my team-mates at Roker Park. Charlie Hurley and I became close friends, for example.

Jim Baxter, too, was another good friend when he came down. It was a shock to me, incidentally, to learn that Jim had been freed. He was certainly a first-class player with Sunderland during the time I was there.

But despite my Sunderland friendships, I often ask myself how things would have gone for me if I'd signed for Celtic in the first place. When you're with one or other of the Old Firm, you're always in the public eye. So you've a head start when it comes to a Scotland team place.

Now that I'm with Celtic, everything is piling up on me. There is a vast difference between playing for a club like Celtic and playing for Clyde. The strain with Celtic is much greater. With so many bright youngsters breathing down your neck, you have to be on your toes all the time. With Clyde on the other hand I was an automatic first-team choice.

One of my biggest disappointments in football is that I never got a schools' international honour. I went to St Aloysius College where Rugby was the official game. I had to toe the line and play it too. I was a hooker, and enjoyed it—but I still missed my football. So much so, indeed, that eventually some of us got together a football team to play friendlies against other schools.

I did get a chance to play football more seriously

Two down, one to go . . . Harry Hood springs into the action, but Airdrie 'keeper McKenzie already has the ball safely in his arms.

when I signed for St Roch's—at the age of 14 years and 9 months. Still keen to get a schools' international cap, I finally changed to Holyrood School.

Selected for the school team, I went on to play in an East v. West schools' international trial; scored two goals and seemed well on the way to that cap. But the authorities took a poor view and I was passed over when it was learned that I had played for St Roch's.

Mine is a footballing family. My brother Jackie, who also played for St Roch's and went to Everton for what was then a record fee for a junior, has given me plenty of help. He and I discuss the games I play in and he tells me where he thinks I've failed.

These little things help to make you a better player, and I'm always grateful for any tips, no matter the source.

And you can never stop learning in this game. I've found that with Celtic I don't have to hold the ball as much as I did with Clyde because the pace is faster and the movement off the ball is faster too.

Every game teaches you something different. While I feel that I'm better suited for a midfield role, I've been doing well as a striker and manager Jock Stein can always get the best out of you in the particular role he wants you to play.

When I'm not playing football there is nothing I like better than a game of golf or some salmon and trout fishing. And into the bargain I'm also a keen gardener. But now Celtic is so much a part of me that my one aim is to be a success with them and keep at the top as long as I can.

Celtic's first goal, against Motherwell—and it's Harry Hood taking off to head the ball past 'keeper Peter McCloy.

ANGELO ANQUILLETTI (Milan and Italy): Full-back. A late developer who suddenly emerged during season 1968/9 as a full-back of world class, playing superbly in Milan's winning European Cup run. He won his first cap for Italy in January, 1969, against Mexico, in Mexico City. Born in San Donato, in the region of Milan, on April 25, 1939, Anquilletti was in fact missed both by Milan and Inter, the other great Milanese club. He began with Solbiatese, and didn't join Atalanta, of the First Division, till 1964. In 1966, he went to Milan. Fast, confident, a quick tackler and a ready attacker, he is an exciting specimen of the contemporary, all-purpose, full-back.

JULIO BAYLON (Universitario and Peru): A coloured winger, mostly operative on the right but also capable of playing dangerously on the left. This he showed in the celebrated 2–2 draw which Peru forced away to Argentina in Buenos Aires, to qualify for the 1970 World Cup. Baylon, already well known in South America before that eliminating tournament started, had established himself by the time it finished as one of the most effective strikers of the moment. Needless to say he is fast, with excellent control, and no reluctance to let fly for goal.

COLIN BELL (Manchester City and England): Though he won his first England caps at the end of season 1967/8, this tall, slender, hugely industrious inside-right fully came into his own late in the following season. He played particularly well in Montevideo and Rio on the England tour of South America. A North Easterner, born in Hesleden, Bury discovered him, launched him, then sold him to Manchester City. He played a key part in the Maine Road club's victories in the League Championship of 1967/8 and the FA Cup Final of 1969. Though essentially a link between attack and defence, he can score himself; as he showed in Rio, against Brazil.

ALBERT CHESTERNIJEV (Central Army Moscow and Russia): A centre-half who generally functions as a sweeper-up, the powerful, diligent Chesternijev, doggedly faithful plugger of holes and filler of gaps, captained Russia's 1966 World Cup team at the age of 25. At 21, he had been a reserve to the 1962 team. He remained captain of the team

59

Colin Bell . . . 'hugely industrious'.

★ BRIAN GLANVILLE'S TOP TWENTY ★

which opposed Ireland and Turkey in the 1970 qualifying series. Coming up through Central Army's junior teams, Chesternijev was also an athlete as a boy. He is married to an Olympic ice skater.

ALLAN CLARKE (Leeds United): In June, 1969, Clarke became England's most expensive player when Leeds United paid £165,000 for him. At this time, he had not yet played for the full England team, though he had a most successful match, and a couple of goals, when an England XI beat a Mexico XI earlier in the month, in Guadalajara. Born in the Midlands at Willenhall, he was brought out by Walsall, moved to Fulham, left them for a record £150,000 in June, 1968, moving to Leicester City, when Fulham were relegated. In 1969, just before Clarke moved again, Leicester were relegated in turn, but not before he'd helped them to reach the Cup Final with a fine, right footed (only) goal against West Bromwich Albion; going on to become Player of the Match in the Final itself. This, though Leicester lost. Tall, slender and deceptively languid, he is excellent in the air, and sublimely unharried when the ball reaches him on the ground.

NESTOR COMBIN (Milan and France): This tall, well built centre-forward, of an almost Aztec mien, was in fact born in 1940 in Las Rosas, Argentina. He was signed by Lyon and brought to France on the basis of his French ancestry, which also enabled him to win French international caps, before being sold to Juventus. There, he failed to settle down, but gradually found better form with Varese, who in turn transferred him, after a season, to Torino, in 1966. There he stayed with growing success till the summer of 1969, when he joined Milan, the European Champions. An unpredictable but strong, talented player, capable on his day of winning any game.

LUIS CUBILLA (Nacional and Uruguay): An excellent, compact little outside-right, born on March 28, 1940, who made his name and won his first Uruguayan caps with Penarol of Montevideo. They transferred him to River Plate of Buenos Aires, with whom he had a number of impressive seasons, before going back to Uruguay in season

Salif Keita . . . 'a celebrated example'.

1968/9. This time, however, he joined the other great Montevidean club, Nacional, quickly regaining his place in the international side. Fast and a most elusive dribbler, he can also head goals; as he showed against England in June, 1969.

FLOREA DUMITRACHE (Dynamo Bucharest and Rumania): A centre-forward who came into the Rumanian World Cup team in 1968, at the age of 20. A skilful, well balanced, confident ball player, he coolly scored Rumania's goal against England from the penalty spot in January, 1969, in a 1-1 draw. He is also most dangerous with his head; as Switzerland found to their cost in a World Cup qualifying match.

LEIF ERIKSSON (Oerebero S.K. and Sweden): Inside-forward whose versatile qualities enable him either to strike or to 'create'. Well able to beat a man, the blond Eriksson is also a most intelligent and acute passer of the ball. Born March 20, 1942, and formerly with Djurgardens, he was one of the few outstanding Swedish forwards of his era who did not try their luck abroad. Played a cardinal part in their impressive run in the World Cup eliminators; and in their defeat of Russia in Moscow in August, 1969.

ALBERTO GALLARDO (Sporting Cristal, Lima and Peru): Peruvian international who played a leading role in Peru's qualification for the 1970 World Cup, at the expense of Argentina. Originally a centre-forward, born in Lima on August 2, 1940, he began with the Cristal club, joined Milan in 1964, played for them on tour in South America, but was then lent for two seasons to Cagliari. There, the well built, coloured centre-forward scored only four goals in forty matches, over two seasons. But on his return to Lima and his old club, he began to find his touch again. His left foot is especially strong.

GERSON (Botafogo and Brazil): Midfield inside-forward. Originally with the most popular of all Rio clubs, Flamengo, the clever Gerson was a member of Brazil's 1960 Olympic team, in Rome, when only 18. His career began, in fact, with the Niteroi team, on the bay of Rio; and he stayed in Rio even when Flamengo sold him, in 1964—to Botafogo. Considered a natural successor to Didi,

Pat Jennings . . . 'enormously agile'.

and won in England; but it was Watford of the Third Division, rather than any of the 'fashionable' clubs, who were shrewd enough to sign him. Having quickly shown his qualities with Watford, Jennings joined Spurs in June, 1964. He'd already won his first cap against Wales, that year, at the age of 20, and quickly went on to establish himself in the Irish international team. He was Tottenham's goalkeeper when they won the Cup in 1967.

FRANCIS LEE (Manchester City and England): The late developer *par excellence*. An outside-right by origin, a centre-forward by temperament and recent usage, Lee never played for the England Under 23 side in his Bolton Wanderers days, and won his first full cap at the age of 25, against Bulgaria, at Wembley, in 1968. His success in the international jersey was immediate, his temperament for the great occasion obvious. Since then, he has gone on to establish himself as the most heartening and important 'discovery' made by England since the World Cup of 1966. Blond, stockily built, fast and unfashionably direct, he turned and virtually won England's match against Northern Ireland in Belfast in May, 1969, going on to play impressively on their South American tour. Bolton put him in their League team at 17, sold him to Manchester City for £60,000 in October, 1967. He has won Cup and League medals with City. Born Bolton.

GERD MULLER (Bayern Munich and West Germany): The centre-forward whom West Germany anxiously sought to succeed Uwe Seeler. That he has something of the same combative spirit Muller showed when he played on in one international match with a broken arm. Though he has still to develop Seeler's calm in the face of provocation; as he showed when he retaliated and won himself months of suspension in season 1968/9. This did not stop him, however, from easily leading the Bundesliga's goal scorers. Tremendously powerful in the thighs and good in the air, he scored, very skilfully, Germany's vital equalising goal in their World Cup eliminating match in Glasgow, that same season.

KEITH NEWTON (Blackburn Rovers and England): A full-back who can play on either flank, Newton has risen above the disadvantages of playing

he was a member of Brazil's 1966 World Cup XI, playing in the match against Hungary—without much success.

SALIF KEITA (St Etienne and Mali): For many years now French football clubs have obtained some of their finest talent from Africa. Keita is a celebrated example. St Etienne brought this tall, slim, long-legged centre-forward from Mali in 1968, and he went almost instantly into their League team. There, even the muddy conditions could not prevent him showing his skills, and he quickly established himself as one of the most gifted, effective forwards in French football. He was born at Bamako, Mali, on December 6, 1946, and joined St Etienne from the club of that name.

PAT JENNINGS (Tottenham Hotspur and Northern Ireland): A tall, well built, enormously agile and brave goalkeeper; with Harry Gregg, the best Ireland has had since Elisha Scott. A much slighter Jennings first drew attention playing for Ireland in the European Youth tournament, held

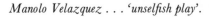

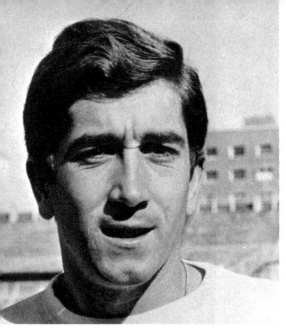

vital World Cup eliminating games. He had a particularly fine match against the Irish in Belfast, when he not only made use of his exceptional height to cut out one high centre after another, but showed courage and anticipation in leaving his goal.

COLIN STEIN (Rangers and Scotland): A centre-forward who cost Rangers £100,000 when they signed him from Hibernian in 1968, Stein has emerged as a striker effective both in club and international football. Those who saw it won't readily forget the splendid leap and header with which he got Scotland's goal against England, at Wembley, in May, 1969. A well built, brave player who won his first caps for Scotland that season, which he concluded by scoring four out of eight goals against Cyprus, at Hampden Park.

MANOLO VELAZQUEZ (Real Madrid and Spain): A blond, versatile, industrious inside-forward who, after several good seasons for Real, fully established himself in 1968/9 as one of their outstanding players. In every sense a product of Real Madrid, he was a member of their fan club as a child and idolised Di Stefano and Kopa. At 22, he was a member of the Real Madrid team which regained the European Cup in 1966, and he has played many times for his country.

in the Second Division to improve steadily as an international player. By the England South American tour of 1969, he was showing the highest class, both at right-back, in Mexico City, and left-back, in Rio. Born in Manchester, but a development of Blackburn Rovers, this tall, powerful player—his tackle is notably strong—says that he owes much to the encouragement of Alf Ramsey. First capped 1966 v Germany and Scotland.

ODILON POLLEUNIS (St Trond and Belgium): Nothing could have been more providential for Belgium than the sudden emergence, at the very time of the World Cup qualifying competition, in 1968, of Polleunis. First he played as a striker against Finland, and scored three goals. Then he dropped back into midfield for the important match at home to Yugoslavia; and promptly got another two. No player did more to qualify Belgium for Mexico than this versatile, effective finisher. He prefers, by the way, to play in midfield. No wonder he became Belgian Footballer of the Year for 1968.

RUDAKOV (Kiev Dynamo and Russia): When Lev Yachine retired from the Russian goal he had graced so long, there were various talented pretenders to his throne. Among them were Psenitchnikov and Kazavachviki, both of whom had their outstanding games. But in the event it was the Kiev goalkeeper, Rudakov, who won the position for the

Days of the individual are ended

By WLODZIMIERZ LUBANSKI

(Gornik Zabrze and Poland)

BORN in the mining village of Sosnice in the heart of the Silesian coalfields I would certainly have gone down the pit like my father if it hadn't been for football. But at 23 I've been around South America twice, played in almost every country in Europe and still got a lot more travelling to do—as long as I keep scoring goals.

At school I was as much interested in athletics as I was football, sprinting in the summer helping me to stay fit for football. Even now I can still do 100 metres in 10.9 seconds which isn't bad for a fellow carrying $11\frac{1}{2}$ stone.

When I was 11 I started to play for the boys' team of GKS Gliwice, a Second Division club, and at 14 it was more or less settled for me that football was to be the most important thing in my life, when I was chosen to play for Poland in the UEFA Youth tournament.

During my second season in the Youth team it seemed that every club in Southern Poland was anxious to sign me but Gliwice have a special arrangement with Gornik—the Miners' Club of Zabrze and soon after my 16th birthday I was transferred to them.

Almost at once I was pushed into the first team and before I'd finished one full season in the First Division I found myself playing in a full international.

Even at the time I knew I had nothing to be big-headed about for there were times when I was completely lost and looking back I know I owe a great deal to Ernst Pohl, captain and inside-left of Gornik when I joined them, and the best player I ever had alongside me. For Gornik and the National team Pohl was always coming to me, looking for a pass when I had the ball, and many a time he 'talked' me out of trouble when I was in possession.

My little bit of talent, and being a bit quick off the mark, was enough when playing alongside Pohl and I learned an awful lot in my five-year apprenticeship with him. Amongst the foreigners who have impressed me most was Ferenc Puskas and I would dearly have liked to play with him—even if it was only once.

Training, of course, is the secret behind the success story of every player, particularly today, when the game is so much quicker than it was even five years ago. I have to train specially hard at the beginning of the season for I seem to take longer than most players to reach my best form.

With Gornik we train particularly hard—maybe that's why we have the best record amongst Polish teams during the last few years. If we have only one match at the week-end we normally train five times each week. Three of the sessions will be long and hard, though usually we do almost everything with the ball.

When training is over, Pohl and I used to go on for an extra half-hour's shooting practice—lobbing balls to each other in turn from different angles and shooting first time with the left and right foot.

It's all been well worthwhile, however, for in 1968/9 I was top scorer in Poland (22 goals) for the second time. Two years ago Polish newspapers began calling me 'our Eusebio' apparently because I resembled the Benfica star when I was running with the ball. I don't think this was a fair comparison at all because I realise how much I've learned—and changed as a result—during the last few years; and I'm still learning now.

When I was 15 or 16 I used to be a bit lazy and selfish, just hanging around near the goal waiting for the scoring chances and playing far too much as an individual. Now I'm trying to take part in a collective team game, switching positions and trying to help my colleagues in possession by running to draw opposing defenders away.

With luck and freedom from any serious injuries I think I can go on improving for another five or six years. I learned the hard way that you can't play as an individual any more and this is specially true of the goalscorers who are always closely marked and followed everywhere. Playing for Gornik doesn't help either, for in Poland we are the team that everyone wants to beat.

Week after week we have to play Cup Finals, knowing that our opponents will get extra big bonuses if they beat us. Inevitably this seems to lead

Wlodzimierz Lubanski in action for Gornik . . . 'Being a bit quick off the mark was enough'.

to more kicking and punching. So far I've been lucky escaping the more serious injuries but have had plenty of bruises. But the best treatment for injuries is to score goals.

My biggest disappointment so far was our failure to reach the last 16 and qualify for the World Cup in Mexico. I had set my heart on it and I thought we really had a good chance but Bulgaria beat us by one point.

Looking at our performances critically, the Polish players have good technique and play the game hard but we have no really outstanding stars to make the team tick. With a Puskas or a Bobby Charlton it might be different but our main problem is that we take too long building up from defence to attack. We also need more international contacts at every level and especially we need more foreign trainers to bring new ideas into our game as Dr Kalocsai did for my team Gornik, and Jaroslav Vejvoda (now back with Dukla Prague) after two years with Legia Warsaw.

The best defenders I've met playing against foreign teams are Bobby Moore of England, Karl Schnellinger from AC Milan and Russia's Khurtsilava. We have one almost as good as them here in Poland in Jacek Gmoch of Legia who always seems to get the better of me. I don't know how or why but he seems to know exactly what I'm going to do—even before I know myself.

Our biggest problem in Poland is financial, as I think it is in most Central and East European countries. We have an awful lot of good young players on the way up but I'm sure that the present generation of players could have achieved better results. Personally I've always been very satisfied with Gornik. I train hard and play hard and in seven years I've never even thought of asking for a transfer.

But the game in Poland is in a kind of twilight zone—an in-between state—neither amateur nor professional. In my opinion the players get enough to live well, but they get more from the game than they put into it. What we need is more dedication and a really serious attempt to play the kind of fast, direct football we saw from England in the 1966 World Cup.

The English, it seems to me, play hard but generally fair. That's what I'd like for our game at home, and for myself I'd like to help Gornik win the European Cup; to keep my place in the national team and qualify for the 1974 World Cup; to go on scoring goals—and to stay out of hospital!

'I was top scorer in Poland for the second time . . .'—and here Lubanski heads one of them in great fashion.

GETTING THAT

EXTRA SPEED

IS A TOUGH JOB

By Gerd Muller

(FC Bayern Munchen and West Germany)

ACCORDING to the English 'Football is a man's game' and though it helps a lot if the man is skilled and intelligent it remains true that the game's excitement is centred on the goal-mouth scrambles, the shots that rebound off the crossbar and, above all, the goals which keep the fans coming. This is the basis of professional football everywhere and in my opinion any player or club not accepting this principle will not stay in the top bracket for long.

The game now is quick and getting quicker; hard and getting harder; and if anyone asks why I am successful where perhaps more skilled players have failed to make the grade, I think its probably due to my far-from-easy upbringing, which gave me the right attitude towards it all.

Born in a tiny Bavarian village a few months after the last war ended I was too young to remember the really hard times my parents had to face. Zinsen, the village where I was born in November 1945 was small and drab. I know it was small because we had no football team, and I had to ride seven miles on a bus to nearby Nordlingen just to get a trial when I was 14. Until then all my football experience had been limited to kick-about games on a bit of level ground at Zinsen.

My father died when I was 15 and I was apprenticed to a weaver. I worked hard at it and really tried to be interested, but most of my time was spent dreaming of becoming a professional footballer. I couldn't afford to buy even a pair of football boots or a jersey in those days—and for my trial match with TSV Nordlingen I had to borrow a pair of boots from a friend. Fifteen years old, and playing on a real pitch for the first time in my life, I scored two goals and the club decided to sign me on.

Why allow pitches such as these?

I owe a great deal to Mr Munzinger, the trainer of the Nordlingen Youth team. It was he who bought me my first pair of boots—out of his own pocket—and he not only made me work extra hard in training but also gave me a great deal of good advice. I remember very clearly him telling me, 'There are players who look good with the ball, but those that really count are the ones able to concentrate, and willing to chase everything. Absolute concentration and dedication from the first second to the last makes the difference between a real centre-forward and a player who just wears a nine on his back.'

I've often had cause to remember this advice. Time after time vital points are won and lost with last-second goals and I remember scoring the only goal in the Cyprus-West Germany World Cup game in 1967. I was in the shower after the match when the contingent of German journalists came into the dressing room and told me that I had scored in the 94th minute!

Every time I recall that match against Cyprus in Nicosia I can't but wonder how it is that FIFA can allow World Cup games to be played on such pitches. Believe me, the field we used when I was a 12-year-old in Zinsen was like Wembley compared to that pitch in Nicosia. I'm sure the ground there has never had real turf on it, and most of the surface was covered with shingle and small pebbles.

It was at Nordlingen, too, that I had my first taste of senior football. After two years with them

they wanted to play me in their first team—but being only 17 I was too young. According to German FA rules players under 18 can only play in senior football with special permission. By the time this was obtained I had already missed the first ten games but before the season was over I was lucky enough to have scored 46 goals.

During the last few weeks of the season, several of the big German clubs had me watched and our President told me the club had received enquiries from 1860 Munich and FC Nurnberg. Our manager Conny Kraft, was an old Nurnberg player himself and he wanted me to join them. Naturally, I began to feel excited and it was no surprise at all when a car with Munich number plates pulled up outside our house. What did surprise me was the fact that the man who stepped out of the car was an official of FC Bayern Munich, the life-long rivals of 1860.

I was eager to be a professional and Bayern didn't want to watch me or talk about it. They offered me a contract and I signed on the spot for 400 Marks a month . . . about £10 a week.

So the country boy from Schwaben moved to the big city, Munich, and at first I had a terrible time. Always a little tubby I have to train extra hard to get fit. My nickname is 'Dicker' . . . 'Fatty' in English. I broke my arm in my first game for Bayern's reserves.

Two months later the Bayern coach, the former Yugoslav international Zlatko Cajkovski, 'Tchik' to all the fans, gave me a chance in the first team. Logically he put me in for the right game, against one of the weaker teams, Freiburger FC. We won very easily by 11-2. Most important for me I got a couple of goals myself, but I had a very hard time settling down in the first team.

The first couple of months were really difficult for although I managed to score a goal now and again I found it almost impossible to play against faster and more experienced players who were close-marking me. Time after time, passes and centres aimed at me were being intercepted and at times it seemed to me that I was never going to make it.

I was too slow. Sure, I went to meet the ball instead of waiting for it to come to me, but though I was beaten by the tiniest fractions of seconds, I was too slow.

'Above all, it's the goals which keep the fans coming' say Gerd Muller: Here he scores with a fine header for Bayern against Belgium's Standard Liege.

Hour after hour of extra training—hitting the ball hard and quick—slowly brought about an improvement. The following season, Bayern won promotion to the Bundesliga and little by little the entire team began to improve and in the last four years we've won almost everything—the German FA Cup; the European Cup Winners' Cup; then the Bundesliga; and finally in 1968/9, the Cup and League double.

For me personally things have gone better than I ever hoped and twice, in 1967 and 1969, I have been voted Footballer of the Year in Germany. Without any false modesty I can say I'm a goalscorer—a tough job in a tough business—and winning that award gives me confidence that I'm doing my job. It is not at all a one man affair—putting the ball in the back of the net is a team matter.

But my job in the team is to round-off everyone else's hard work. That is why I feel that being top-scorer in the Bundesliga and being Footballer of the Year is important because scoring goals is my business and if I stop getting goals it means I'm failing.

WORLD'S COSTLIEST PLAYER —AND I DIDN'T KNOW IT!

By PIETRO ANASTASI (Juventus and Italy)

in an interview with Geoff Parkin

I'LL never forget the night I became the world's most expensive footballer in a straight cash deal of £410,000. It was a transfer which caused a sensation throughout Italy. Yet I was practically the last person to learn about it.

And when the news was broken to me, my very first thought was: 'But the "wrong" club have bought me!'

It came about this way. In May 1968 I had just completed my first season in Division 1, and with the goals coming regularly it had been a very good season for a youngster like myself, a newcomer to this class of Soccer.

For weeks the newspapers had been buzzing with news of the attempts which the big-spending clubs were making to sign me from Varese, who had given me my First Division chance.

When the transfer season opened Inter-Milan were reckoned by everyone to be the favourites for my signature. The negotiations were well advanced and when at the end of May, Varese agreed to loan me to Inter for a friendly match against Roma it looked as though the deal was all tied-up.

As I ran out of the tunnel in the Inter strip the fans gave me a great reception. And when the breaks came my way and I scored twice during the first half they really turned it on.

In the dressing room during the interval I received congratulations from the lads I was convinced would be my future team-mates and naturally I felt pretty good.

The first hint I got about my real destination was when a crowd of Press photographers rushed over and started shooting off flash bulbs right, left, and centre as we came out for the second half.

When I asked in bewilderment what all the fuss was about, one of the photographers drew me on one side and asked me: 'But haven't you heard? Juventus have just signed you for a world record fee of six hundred and twenty million Lire!'

There wasn't time to ask any more. The match was re-starting. I don't remember much about the second half. The fact which put me in a turmoil was not the colossal figure involved, but that my new club was Juventus. I had already conditioned myself mentally to becoming an Inter player.

Afterwards the news was confirmed by the Varese directors and I adjusted quickly to the situation.

I can honestly say, however, that the label of the

The sort of moment that helped make him the world's costliest footballer: A goal for Juventus from Pietro Anastasi.

world's costliest footballer has not had any influence on my play. I hope this doesn't sound like conceit. The truth is that I am so wrapped-up in football and enjoy it so much that when I get out onto the field I just forget everything except the match on hand. And I am willing to bet that nearly every other player would tell you exactly the same thing.

Believe me I fully realise how lucky I have been in Soccer. I came from a working-class family in the suburbs of Catania in Sicily, and was one of hundreds of kids who spent all their spare time kicking a ball around. I had a couple of seasons with Fourth Division amateurs Massiminiana and my first stroke of luck was being brought North by Varese straight into the First Division.

I was lucky again there in finding team-mates who helped me develop and were truly unselfish in giving me the breaks which enabled me to score the goals which attracted the attention of the big clubs.

Lucky again on my transfer to Juventus. Instead of having the entire summer to think about it, I was called up to play in the Italian National team in the finals of the European Nations Cup and this kept me busy when I needed it.

In the first match against Jugoslavia I had a very indifferent game. But in the replay of the final I scored Italy's second goal in their 2–0 win and this gave me confidence.

Where I really needed luck was in my first League season with Juventus. And Lady Luck didn't let me down. The goals still kept coming, and the transition period went smoothly. I know that if I had struck a bad patch then the fans and the critics would have been merciless and it could have destroyed me.

Now I am established among the highest-priced and best-paid players in the country. And I willingly accept the sacrifices that being in this category demands.

Early nights, with bedtime at around ten o'clock, watching the diet, and spending hours training to keep oneself in absolute peak condition every week of the year are the part of a footballer's life that is accepted without thinking about it. Other youngsters of my age—I was born on April 7, 1948—can have the high-life.

Give me the thrill of running out on to the pitch with a ball at my feet, and 60,000 fans packed on the terraces just waiting to unleash the roar that rocks the whole stadium whenever I slam the ball into the net.

That's the moment when a £410,000 price tag, with all the responsibility it carries, sinks into insignificance.

DI STEFANO

By STRATTON SMITH

(Editor, International Football Book)

chester United, entering the competition for the first time, had reached the semi-final of the 1956/7 European Cup. United were the most creative and loved team in Britain. Disillusion persisted with the England national team and its policies, still wounded by the Hungarian defeats of three years before. But the luminous purity of United's and Busby's methods would now re-affirm at club level that British was best.

Or would they? Busby's own uncalculated realism and generous praise for Real Madrid quickly dampened all talk of a 'walk over'. Students of Matt Busby noted a certain strain in his normally-cordial public persona at Madrid's El Fenix Hotel before the game. The Press, as if evaluating for the first time the simple fact that Real Madrid were the European Cup-holders (after all, there it was, on display in the club-room), switched to a line that this would be a 'Classic encounter'.

So it proved; and if any one man made it so, it was Alfredo di Stefano. White is the mnemonic of that day at Bernabeu: an eruption of white flowers and handkerchiefs and roars so great, sound seemed transmuted into light, a light which passed through

LITTLE over a dozen years ago foreign football seemed to be played in a continuous dense fog for all that was seen and known of it in Britain. Thus when Matt Busby returned from his first viewing of Real Madrid and said flatly 'I have never seen a better player than Di Stefano' the reaction here was of surprise, apprehension, and 'Who the heck is Di Stefano?'

Di Stefano himself soon changed all that. Man-

'His closest friend in British football was also his first, great opponent, Sir Matt Busby': Sir Matt welcomes Di Stefano at Manchester Airport.

the white shirts of Real and hit United like a laser beam. True, United were out of luck. But by the end, too, they were out of steam, close to being hypnotised by an aggregate of individual skills, experience, and tactics the like of which they had probably never previously met. The return game at Old Trafford, though a draw, only confirmed that, for that year at least, Real were the masters.

Those two games wrote Di Stefano so largely into the literature of British football that his name thereafter could never be forgotten. Nor is it, now that he is retired and a team manager back in his native Argentine. Succeeding years, the many encounters with Di Stefano that followed, taught us much more about both his football and his personality. But the sum of it added little to Matt's spot judgement back in early '57: That Di Stefano is arguably the greatest of post-war players, and possibly the greatest of all time.

As Matt has said, Di Stefano kept play at the level

of 'Win all the time'. Unlike Pelé, perhaps his closest rival for historical supremacy, he was relentless for 90 minutes. Stocky and strong, he had both the body and the intelligence to persuade one that the game flowed through him; he could be, and often was, the pivotal figure in a situation on his own goal-line and seconds later be on the opponent's to complete the same movement he had begun.

Unlike Stanley Matthews, another contender, Di Stefano was sparing of his personal skill. He was rather like a clever financier; he didn't often use his own money because his credit was indisputable. To Di Stefano, strategy and tactics were a more engaging occupation than virtuosity; his game never relapsed into self-indulgence. What he did was to bring into play the money (or rather, skills) of others. If hard work was his characteristic, then probing for space and accurate use of the ball was his genius.

Di Stefano was rarely caught with the ball. He held it, not to try and beat a man, though he could do that brilliantly enough, but to draw out the moment of threat to a defence, to harrass the defender mentally, force him into a move—and make a space. That's why his greatest partnerships

Francisco 'Paco' Gento—'Di Stefano's greatest partnerships ripened with men who were fine runners off the ball'.

The 'Million pound bench'!—Ferenc Puskas, Sir Stanley Matthews, Di Stefano, and Czechoslovakia's Josef Masopust, changing for Sir Stanley's farewell game at Stoke.

ripened with men who were fine runners off the ball —Ferenc Puskas, 'Paco' Gento—rather than fellow ball-players and tacticians such as the Frenchman Raymond Kopa, who had a brief and unhappy period with Real, good player though he was. There could only be one Di Stefano in any team.

The fact that he scored goals—and many a memorable goal, at that—or in terms of skills was one of the most complete players imaginable, these things seemed like icing on the cake. Di Stefano's significance was his utter modernity, his relevance to the 'new football' of the 'whirl' and all-round, unceasing team work. Hidegkuti of Hungary had preceded him—in Europe, at least—as a deep-lying centre-forward of great power and effectiveness, but overall, and possibly because I saw more of Di Stefano, I think the Real Madrid man was the better all-round player.

In the early '60s, I had the opportunity of spending a week or two with Pelé in Santos and a similar period with Di Stefano in Spain—he had by then moved to Barcelona Espanol. The dignified minds of both men and their intense interest in their profession impressed me greatly. Yet the mind of the one lacked the steel of the other. In football terms, Di Stefano was a man of steel. Variably warm or aloof, quick-tempered off-field yet remarkably cool on it, young-minded (happily turned on to The Beatles because his children liked them, and a close friend of 'Beatle' matador El Cordobes), Di Stefano has left me with a lasting impression of professionalism, intelligence, and dignity. He graced this game of football in more ways than one, and it is not unexpected that his closest friend in British football was also his first, great opponent—Sir Matt Busby.

Lack of temperament is France's problem

By SALIF KEITA

(Saint Etienne, Champions of France, and Mali)

BORN in Mali at a time when the country was a French colony, and playing for Saint Etienne, Champions of France, for the last four years in a row, I feel myself to be part of the French game and yet not a Frenchman.

'My boss Albert Batteaux built my confidence' says Keita, here being hugged by the Saint Etienne chief; (right) Keita shows some of that confidence in winning a tussle with the Bordeaux defence.

Until I came to France the greater part of my life was spent in Bamako, the capital of Mali, and to be

More Top of the Shots than Top of the Pops—but anyway, England's World Cup squad tried their hand at recording their 'Back Home' theme song in a London studio.

more precise the Bamako suburb of Ouaofobougou. The nearest open fields were miles away and wide streets just didn't exist. We used to play between the rows of shacks and tumbledown houses and the biggest open area we could find was a little 'square' 20 yards by 10 yards.

No enchiladas and burritos for England's men in Mexico— they 'bridged that gap' with good old-fashioned (sic) beefburgers, flown from home . . .

I hadn't even touched a pair of football boots, let alone worn any, when one evening a man came knocking on the door asking for 'Domingo'. Keita is my family name, and I was christened Salif but in Mali I was always known by my nickname . . . 'Domingo'.

The man explained he was from the Football Association and that he'd seen me play in our 'square'. Mali had to send a team to Indonesia for an international tournament and with illness and injuries they were short of players, 'Would you like to go?' the man asked me, 'And can you be ready to-morrow morning?'

It all seemed so unreal, totally unbelievable. Here was I, a boy who had rarely ridden on a bus *flying* halfway round the world! The FA gave me a pair of boots and our team had so few players that I played two games on that trip, and before I returned home to Bamako officials of Real Bamako had signed me on.

Playing and training facilities in Mali are not good. We trained three times a week on bone-hard grounds after work, usually between 6 and 7.30 p.m. There isn't much hope that these facilities will improve much in the next decade or so for there are greater priorities like hospitals and schools and roads. Football comes way down the list of items recommended for government expenditure but even so I am sure there will be many more African players who make their mark in the European game.

In my case there were many reasons that brought me to France. First because French was the only European language that I understood but most of all I think I had a deep desire to prove myself as a player. In Mali I was accepted as a star player too easily, and I wanted more than that. Finally the decision was made. I was going to St Etienne.

I had saved some money and just managed to scrape together enough for a one-way ticket to Paris but when I landed at Orly airport I had only ten Francs (about 15 shillings) and my friend's advice —get a taxi. The first taxi-driver just laughed when I asked him to take me to the ground of Saint Etienne.

The second pointed out that it was more than 300 miles from Paris to Saint Etienne but finally I managed to find one taxi driver who was willing to take me and I slept that night curled up in the taxi. Next morning we arrived at the ground of Saint Etienne and after lengthy explanations and discussions, the Club Secretary paid the taxi bill of about £80 and found me lodgings.

The first year with Saint Etienne was full of difficulties for me. I had to get used to the closer marking and quicker tackling and I was understudy for the Algerian inside-forward, Rachid Mekloufi. Finally when he took on the job of player-manager for Bastia in Corsica I got my chance.

It hasn't been as difficult as I expected—two seasons brought me two Championship medals and already I've played in half the countries of Europe. Playing on mud and snow wasn't as big a problem as I expected. Being slightly built and having good balance I seem to have an advantage over opponents in slippery conditions.

I owe an awful lot to Saint Etienne and in particular my boss Albert Batteux who has done so much to build up my confidence and develop my ability. Heading was a great weakness in my play when I left Mali but under Batteux's patient coaching I am very much better now.

Three times in a row Saint Etienne have been Champions of France and three times we have failed to make any real progress in the European

Cup. More than anything else M. Batteux wants us to do well and last season when we eliminated the German champions Bayern Munchen—with Beckenbauer and Muller—we really thought we had overcome most of our problems. But it was not to be.

Living amongst Frenchmen and playing against teams from Italy, Germany, and Britain I can sense the difference in attitude. AC Milan, Celtic, Manchester United, Ajax and Bayern are the best teams I've seen and played against and they all have something that is difficult to explain but which is certainly lacking in French football.

To overcome them, the French need to meet them more often to gain experience and confidence, but right down, deep at the heart of the problem, is a question of temperament which the French just have not got.

Salif Keita dwarfs São Paulo's Lucas as he strides away during a friendly with the Brazilian club.

FOOTBALL—FOR LOVE OR MONEY?

By DRAGAN DZAJIC

(Red Star, Belgrade and Yugoslavia)

WHEN I was young my teachers at school and my parents wanted me to go to University. I myself always liked the idea of being a teacher and though the manager of Red Star, Belgrade, persuaded my parents to let me be a footballer instead, I sometimes have regrets.

There is a big consolation though, because while I became a professional player for Red Star (Crvena Zvezda in our language) I carried on with my studies. Passing my examinations I am already a student teacher and I stay in football for a variety of reasons.

First, because I really do enjoy playing as I always have, and secondly because the money I am earning gives me a good living and my future is secure. How much longer I will stay in the game is a difficult question and my thoughts on this point vary almost from week to week.

There are times—for example when I played for the World XI against Brazil in Rio de Janeiro—when I feel really good and would like to go on playing for ever. Looking around the FIFA team dressing-room that day I felt an enormous sense of achievement that I was thought to be good enough to play with men who are household names around the world. That was good. But there are other times when I feel really ashamed to be a footballer and in this mood I'm almost ready to quit the game altogether.

(Above) Dzajic the student teacher—(right) Dzajic (striped shirt) the Soccer star . . . 'But there are times when I'm ashamed to be a footballer'.

Looking at myself critically, I believe myself to be educated and calm and I am aware that I should behave as a gentleman . . . on the field and off it. I'm a real professional from head to foot. I work hard in training, go to bed early, live to a strict diet, and don't drink. I know my personal friends seem to have a better life, they can eat and drink all they want and enjoy themselves.

Non-smoking, and playing for a club with high standards of discipline and training, I feel I earn my big bonuses, which at times are equal to three months pay for an ordinary worker. But I know my future depends on it and I have to sell my talent while it lasts. When I quit I'll become a teacher full-time and I know that I'll have to compete then for promotion against people who have a head start on me, with years of experience behind them.

For the moment I'm a professional footballer, really trying to play as well as I can, but I know it can't go on much longer. One day I'll feel so badly after a game that I'll just suddenly quit. Unless you've been in my position it's almost impossible to understand.

I enjoy playing, I think it's still a great game and I go on to the pitch aware that people have paid hard earned money to see me and 21 others play. I do my best to entertain, but you just cannot imagine the tremendous pressures.

When I played for Yugoslavia against Belgium in Brussels—a match that really eliminated us from the 1970 World Cup—it was terrible. In the first minute—before I'd even touched the ball I had already been kicked and punched! Of course, my assailants made sure the referee was looking the other way at the time.

Even without the ball I was getting kicked . . . so

'I do my best to entertain, but you can't imagine the pressures': Dzajic weaves past two Olimpia defenders in a League game in Ljubliana.

often I lost count of the number of times. Finally I lost control and retaliated. The referee saw that and sent me off. I sat in the dressing-room absolutely ashamed.

I know I shouldn't have retaliated, and I realise too that my colleagues often deliberately foul opponents but I realise that behind all the increasing violence is the bigger and bigger bonuses being paid . . . *if you win*. This is the basis of professionalism.

I still believe that the star players are those with the real talent and intelligence—players who can think while the game goes on and change the rhythm of the game, slowing it down, and then suddenly at just the right moment speeding it up again.

They must have the ability to improvise in tight situations, to create through their skill a good position out of nothing. Such players are the foundation of the game. But they are also the prime targets for their opponents and I can't see any really top-class player staying in the game for long.

As a youngster matures and reaches star quality,

he'll cash in quick, make a lot of money and get out of the game before he is seriously injured.

Knowing this, I cannot be anything but pessimistic about the future of the game for it is these stars—the key men—who the fans pay to see and yet opponents, managers and players alike, edicated themselves to stopping the star from playing. It all comes down to a question of money.

Thirty years ago the players played for peanuts and enjoyed every minute of it. Sure there were a few tough players about—there always will be—but the majority of the players at that time, loved the game and played because they liked it. This is still true for the youngster today.

He plays football because he enjoys it and the best of them are fired with ambition and want to become stars. It's only when you get into the game and begin to feel the terrible pressures being exerted against you, that you become aware that the future of the game itself is really black.

As an entertainment the game cannot possibly

Tough moment at Crystal Palace—goalkeeper John Jackson meets resistance from Chelsea's Tommy Baldwin as he tries to punch this one away . . .

last much longer. Even in Yugoslav League games, these pressures exist. Being the Champions, we are the team everyone wants to beat.

They are promised big bonuses and the opposing manager tells his players to kick the key men. It isn't a sport any more. It's a business—brutal and hard.

At some time in the not-too-distant future the fans will decide that what passes for football isn't really football at all, but a miniature war and not many civilised people will want to watch it. When that day comes the game will die.

Look at it logically. The 'ideal' team is a goal-keeper and five really tough defenders—players like Stiles—and for the attack five like Bobby Charlton. But the defenders aim to cancel out the talented men and it has always been easier to destroy things rather than create. It's easy to burn down an art gallery with a petrol bomb but it takes real talent to paint the pictures.

From my personal experience, big money is the real problem facing the game. The more money there is in it for the players, the tougher the game becomes. I would love to play in real, honest football —but the atmosphere within the game and the pressures on the players make this impossible. Time after time I sit in the changing-room after a tough game and I feel ashamed to be a part of it.

WEMBLEY
6 : 3

BUDAPEST
7 : 1

IT'S HUNGARY'S TURN TO LEARN

By KAROLY SOOS
(Hungary's national team manager)

FOOTBALL, like everything else in life is constantly changing, developing as a result of new ideas, new training methods; speeded up by the ever increasing popularity of the game and the incessant demands for victory. Of course, something has to suffer and in football it is the entertainment aspect of the game which has paid the price.

But while many critics don't like the new game which is evolving we have no choice but to accept it . . . and work harder. Football today is not so nice to watch, except perhaps in friendly matches, but it is today faster than ever, more powerful and making greater demands in every sense on the players.

Not many years ago it was enough if a player was good with the ball but today the individual must adapt his talents to the needs of his team and the demands of the modern game.

In Western Europe, where professionalism is most advanced, there was always more physical contact between the players. This remains true today, but more heavily emphasised as the game becomes harder and tougher. In South America it's not all the same. There football is still an entertainment

Hungary's great centre-forward, Florian Albert.

above all else and the skill of the individual is what the fans want to see . . . except maybe in Argentina. There as in Europe, the players make greater use of their bodies.

The game is still good, and can be exciting, too, but in a new, different way. Not long ago everyone was playing to the WM style or 4–2–4 pattern but now the game is dominated by a new system. What many people fail to realise is that each different system calls for different qualities but at the heart of it all is basic skill.

Today the players must have skill, but whereas they could become a star on that alone not long ago, today they must be very well coached in order to make the maximum use of their skills. At the moment we are in a kind of half-way house; caught between a system of play which called for players who special-ised in playing in one position . . . and the new game now developing which makes even greater demands on the players, required to attack and defend in turn.

They are now required to be multi-purpose players, not just left-backs and right-halves, but all-rounders who can take part in a team game and do any job that needs doing as the occasion arises!

As I see the future of the game, in the highest class all the players will be multi-purpose players; attack-ing and defending in turn. The days of the great individual stars are over; we've seen Pelé and Eusebio, Di Stefano and Best—and the emphasis now is on team-work. Do the simple things quickly, do them well and run, run, run.

Managers of national teams have a really hard time because such players need to work constantly together with their coach to develop the necessary understanding and of course 95% of their time the players spend training with their own clubs. In Hungary this problem is underlined because our players following the national characteristics have always tended to be independent and individual.

As I see it the Hungarian game is today living on its reputation earned in the past. Our players and fans still remember beating England twice in the 1953–4 season 6–3 at Wembley and 7–1 in Buda-pest. In Hungary we are still looking back when we should be working for the future. The English who were on the receiving end of these great victories

The best examples of the modern game are seen in England and West Germany' says Karoly Soos. English 'fighting spirit' is here exemplified by Watford's Barry Endean, embroiled with the Liverpool defence . . .

And again it's giant-killing Watford—with Tom Walley (light shirt) leaving the runway alongside Liverpool's Ron Yeats

back in the 'fifties have learned the lessons from those defeats and as a result they improved enormously.

Perhaps the best examples of the modern game are seen in England and West Germany and it is on these teams that we in Hungary must base our new style of play. We must do it, but without losing any of our individual technique. The Hungarian ability, combined with better physical condition and fighting spirit would be really great.

But we face one really great problem. We are not professionals. Ask the players to work harder, to attain better condition in terms of stamina and speed and the typical Hungarian will shrug his shoulders and, say: 'I am only an amateur'. Our players cannot accept my conviction that we must be harder and more determined in our approach. There is one basic truth in football—that individual technique can only be expressed when our team has the ball.

In Hungary our problems resolve into this: We must get possession before we can demonstrate our skill and the players are not prepared to 'fight' for the ball.

The South Americans, Brazil being a prime example, refuse to accept this fact as a truth of the modern game and I believe this was why they failed so badly in the 1966 World Cup. In Rio de Janeiro the game is just a show—a super spectacular. But in Brazil, Hungary, and everywhere else life itself is faster now. It is more and more difficult to make a living for the individual and the nation.

Our coaches recognise these facts and with regular meetings with our top coaches I know the problems are understood. The game is so fast now that there is no time for showing off, beating an opponent when it is not necessary. We must work at simple, basic things . . . things that look simple and seem simple but are in fact very difficult to develop in players.

The game of the future . . . and that starts tomorrow . . . revolves around players with a high degree of skill allied to intelligence and excellent physical condition. Only players with all these qualities can take part in the new game which hinges on a continuous changing of position (by the players) and a rapid circulation of the ball.

Looking around the world I have seen *some* players who can already play this game: players like Beckenbauer and Muller of West Germany; Prati in Italy and Peters in England. But I couldn't name a complete XI . . . even with the whole world to choose from. This demonstrates the magnitude of the problem.

This new game demands so much and is so much more difficult to play. Youngsters in my day regarded football as a pleasure (which it was). They all wanted to be big stars. But today football means hard work, real *hard work*, and young men have begun to look around for other pastimes, other sports, which they can enjoy without the need for really hard work.

We are not alone with this problem in Hungary. Take France as a typical example. The French game has been in decline for some years because people want an easier life. Youngsters want to enjoy their lives and the emphasis is on seeking pleasure. They can find it too . . . but not in football.

There are few players more determined than Wolves' Derek Dougan, here going into the crunch with two Stoke defenders.

By OSCAR MAS
(River Plate and Argentine)

I was as shocked as everyone else that little countries like Peru and Bolivia should get the better of us. Certainly it shouldn't have happened and I am quite positive that if we were to play the two teams again we would beat them. It was just one of those things . . . like that 'United States 1, England 0' scoreline which staggered everyone in the 1950 World Cup in Brazil.

But obviously, when a good team loses, then some-

WE DON'T DESERVE THIS NAME FOR 'DIRTY PLAY'

ONE of the features about football which gives it widespread appeal is the fact that there is no such thing as a foregone conclusion. If every game resulted in the way that the form book indicated, then every fan would win the pools (or Toto or Lotto) every week and the grounds would be empty. Excitement, tension, surprise, and luck all combine to make it possible *sometimes* for the giants to lose to the minnows.

When the draw was announced for the 1970 World Cup qualifying competition everyone I know said 'O.K. that's a pushover'. No one doubted even for one minute that we wouldn't murder Peru and annihilate the Bolivians. Taking things for granted is one of the biggest weaknesses in human nature and preparing for a match with an 'unbeatable' attitude is begging for disaster.

This is the closest I can go to giving an explanation for the fact that Argentina finished bottom of the group.

River Plate's Oscar Mas (white shirt) in action—'I'm a little fellow who plays an attacking game . . . dirty play doesn't suit me'.

one must take the blame and in this case it is impossible for me to blame the players, the manager, or the FA. Everyone in the Argentinian game must accept their share of responsibility—the clubs, the players, the FA, and the State.

After the event, when Peru had qualified, all the critics emphasised how hard the Peru squad had worked for their victory and how amateurish we had been by comparison. Of course Didi knew he had to work very hard with his players and on and off Didi and his chosen squad were kept together for long periods.

For the best part of ten months Peru prepared while we and the Bolivians just called a handful of players together a week before the first game. Of course our efforts by comparison were feeble, but those same journalists who criticised us all after we had lost were the very people who were writing . . . 'It's O.K.—We'll murder them!'

In the past our Argentinian squad has often been put together just days before big competitions and done well because the players were good as individuals and were able to blend with each other's game.

A typical example of this is illustrated by Argentina's results in 1957/8. A young and inexperienced team was put together and flew off to Lima, Peru, to play in the South American Championship.

All the experts were critical; the team had no class, no experience—and yet the results they achieved surprised everyone. We beat Uruguay by 4-0 and hammered Brazil 3-0 to win the Trophy. Then the following year, with Uruguay failing to qualify, both Argentina and Brazil went to Sweden for the 1958 World Cup and what happened? Did we hammer Brazil again and cover ourselves in glory? Of course not. The history books show clearly that Argentina got knocked out in the first round while Brazil beat everyone to win the World Cup for the first time!

It doesn't help to change the officials in charge too often and it does no good making panic changes after a defeat either. These perhaps are the most important lessons we must digest here in Buenos Aires. An outstanding leader cannot become an idiot overnight and neither does a great player become a novice after one poor game. But panic changes have so often been made in the past, and it

Oscar Mas skips away from a slide-tackle—'The average Argentinian player is neither an angel nor a devil'.

must be accepted that this played at least some part in explaining Argentina's failure to beat Peru and Bolivia.

Selector-coach, Humberto Maschio, took charge of the preparations in January 1968. A fine player when with Racing, I cannot comment on his ability as a coach or manager because he never picked me for his squad. All I know is that he was a fine player —and he was discharged only a fortnight before the first World Cup game against Bolivia. Only a week before the squad flew off to La Paz, Adolfo Pedernera was appointed to replace Maschio and it was only then that my River Plate colleague Daniel Onega and myself were called up to form a new left wing.

Pedernera I've known a long time, and his record as a coach stands up to the closest scrutiny. Over the last few years he's been used like a one-man fire

Nottingham Forest's Hindley comes through like a tank—and momentarily seems to have stunned Everton's Sandy Brown (left) and Brian Labone.

brigade by the rich clubs who suddenly find themselves in trouble and invariably Pedernera has restored balance and confidence in his team. But even a genius can't work miracles in a fortnight!

It is also true that the attitude of the clubs . . . and the players . . . is not what it might be, for no one relishes the thought of long tours abroad or exhaustive preparations at home in Argentina. The clubs don't like losing their star players for weeks on end and I've often known of clubs who have ordered their players not to turn up for training with the national team because they are afraid their stars might get injured and be unfit to play in a forthcoming League or Cup match.

The fans are naturally indignant when Argentina loses international matches but they don't seem to understand the player's point of view. The way things are set up here in Argentina, the players receive a very small basic salary—but big bonuses for winning. In a month during which three games are lost and one drawn the players might collect, say, £40 for the month, but a month in which the same club wins four games and a friendly game, or international Cup-tie against a Brazilian or Uruguayan team, the pay check for the same player leaps up to maybe £400.

The Argentinian FA and the fans seem to think that playing for our country should be reward nough. I'm always delighted to be chosen and I am positive that this is true of many other players. But while the FA gives the players nothing at all for training sessions and very little incentive bonuses either, the players know only too well that if they break a leg playing for Argentina they might be out of the game for months—perhaps crippled for ever with knee trouble.

One last point I would stress with regard to Argentina and the reputation for dirty play we have become stuck with. I personally dislike rough or dirty play and in any case, being a little fellow who plays an attacking game, it doesn't favour me if a match gets out of hand.

I know there have been some disgraceful matches given wide publicity but I can honestly say that they are not truly representative of Argentinian football. A handful of hot-heads can get a whole country a bad name—as has happened recently.

But playing in Buenos Aires every week and having travelled widely abroad I can assure you, and will insist, that the average Argentinian player is neither an angel nor a devil. He's simply a professional player trying to make a living.

Watford 'keeper Walker dives at the feet of Liverpool's Alun Evans with team-mate Lees on hand to give support.

MY PARTNER, PELÉ!

'The secret is to try and follow his reflexes . . .'

By GERSON SABIDO
(leading Brazilian critic)

TWO or three years ago I did not pay much attention to his game. I considered Tostão an average player, neither better nor worse than any other. Over the years I started to pay more attention to his game. Each time I saw him I thought he improved. Suddenly the explosion . . .

It became apparent here was a player with perfect balance, who never fell, even when barged or tackled. His carrying of the ball and dribbling was different from any other player: he dribbled away from his opponent, that is, on the outside, whereas the average or ordinary player does the opposite.

Furthermore, when carrying the ball he always holds his head high; having therefore complete vision of the field before him and an enormous facility to push the ball around. It astonished me to find that he was everywhere on the ground and seemingly always in the right place at the right time.

Somebody asked me whether I preferred him to Eusébio and my reply was that Tostão was certainly the better man. I thought him better than Albert of Hungary and fast approaching the quality and capability of Bobby Charlton.

In Brazil's national side, Tostão played a big part in the qualification for the Finals in Mexico—scoring 10 of the 23 Brazilian goals against Venezuela,

Eduardo Goncalves de Andrade, 'Tostão': 'Better than Albert of Hungary and fast approaching the capability of Bobby Charlton'.

Colombia, and Paraguay. His brilliant offensive play opened up new tactics for the Brazilian side, whose players are so aggressively minded. His presence on the Brazilian team does not obscure Pelé, but his tactical importance increases, for, while his opponents worry themselves over Pelé and the ball, Tostão scores the goals.

Should they forget Pelé and pay more attention to Tostão, the 'King' then comes into action and scores the necessary goals. For this reason, the Brazilian spectator has suddenly become aware of the appearance of Pelé's ideal partner. Or in other words, the heir-apparent to the throne. This partnership was the missing link in England during the World Cup of 1966.

And what is Pelé's opinion of him? I asked the genius of football and he said:

'Tostão dribbles extremely well, shoots hard, knows how to place himself in readiness for a pass, is excellent in first-time passing due to his accuracy in making the ball reach its destination unerringly. I like the way he covers the entire field always holding his head high. He is always in the right place at the right time, for when a 'keeper kicks away or fumbles, he is always there to collect the ball. As a friend, Tostão is better still. He is modest and friendly to all his colleagues.

'His ability is enormous. His play changed all known concepts of forward play, proving in a positive manner that intelligence and cleverness can beat size and brute force, at least within a football ground.'

Eduardo Gonçalves de Andrade, 'Tostão', is 22 years old, 5 ft 6½ in. tall, and has received every bestowable honour with his club, Cruzeiro FC of Belo Horizonte, during the last four years. He also has the experience of a World Cup Tournament, which Brazil lost in Britain. On that occasion he only played once, in Liverpool against Hungary, when Brazil lost by 3 goals to 1 and Tostão scored his side's only goal: he was 19 at the time.

In conversation with him he told me that in 1966 many things took place: firstly, it can be considered a transitionary period. There were many older players who had given Brazil many glories in the past, in 1958 and 1962, and others were newcomers to the national side, such as himself. Above all, the team lacked organisation. The understanding among players was poor. And, when leaving Brazil, the team already lacked the determination to win.

In my opinion, things have now changed. The understanding is top-rate, the quality of Brazil's game is first-rate. I did not wish to say it, but I felt the 1970 World Cup would be ours. Tostão feels that the new will to win results from the greater maturity at this stage of the Brazilian player.

He dislikes being called the 'White Pelé'. He says

Tostão's shock goal against England at Maracanã. (Top, left) the Brazilian star is down, he thinks he has a touch of cramp . . . but England's Ken Newton is bringing that ball under control very near to Tostão's left foot . . . next shot, he is half-way up, and desperately trying to hook the ball away from Newton; he succeeds, just as Gordon Banks slithers across to try and save (bottom). It has to be a goal . . . the upraised, gesturing arms of Banks and Bobby Moore (above) tell the tale. And they're left in no doubt (below) as Tostão's team-mates leap in to hug him.

A windswept Bobby Moore—'The best of the lot' says Tostão.

area, or in any other part of the field, he is always cool, an opportunist, and calm. His goal against England which made the match a draw is a typical example of the above. He carried the ball towards Ken Newton at speed, and when Newton thought he would try to pass him on the inside, he dribbled him along the sideline and centred firmly for Jairzinho to score.

His understanding with others in the team could not be better. He feels that his understanding with Pelé is so good because he considers him one of the eleven. 'The difficulty of playing with Pelé is his very rapid reflexes. The secret is to try and follow his reflexes. I feel a technical player plays better when he is with Pelé.'

I asked him to compare England's team—which played in Maracanã Stadium before 145,000 spectators—with the Champion team of 1966. He was quite sincere when he said that the current team is much better; the players, he said, have more ability. He was impressed by the English players' admirable technical discipline but comments on the lack of fun in playing in this way. Above all he feels the English team does not go after the goals as it should. When I invited him to mention the outstanding players, he pointed out Bobby Charlton, Alan Mullery and, above all, Bobby Moore—whom he feels is the best of the lot.

Most of Tostão's football is played in the Minas Gerais Stadium, known as 'Mineirao', the capacity of which is 135,000; one of the most modern in the world! He is not of the opinion that playing Soccer is more important than reaching the moon, but he feels that the most important thing is for man to live in peace. He considers Pope John XXIII the outstanding personality of the century in view of the far-reaching changes brought about by him in the Roman Catholic Church.

A few days ago, Tostão mentioned to a Russian journalist, using surprisingly diplomatic tact, that Soccer is one of the means a Capitalistic nation has of approaching a Socialist country. He always has an unexpected answer. He thinks that men within a field reveal themselves, communicate, express themselves and show all they are and feel. Fame has not gone to his head and he has not changed at all in

that sometime in the future Pelé will end his career as a player. At this point it will then be possible to speak of a successor to Pelé. Currently Pelé sacrifices his game; he also plays defensively, marking other players. 'When in an attacking move he is always marked by at least two opposing players and therefore he asked the others to funnel more of their passes to me.'

Pelé, he says, cannot be classed with any other player. After him, a number of players can be classed on equal terms. 'In this group I realise that I am one of the best. Everything I do, however, within a football ground, I realise can be done better. With Pelé things seem a little different; everything he does is perfect!'

Tostão is a natural goal-scorer. Within the goal

Pelé, still 'The King' (inset, right). (Above) Pelé shows his skills in Santos' 3–2 friendly win at Stoke; (below) he cracks in the first of his two goals.

the way he treats people.

He is very fond of João Saldanha, Brazil's team manager, and considers that he possesses a deep knowledge of the game. One of the ills besetting Brazilian football is that everyone thinks himself knowledgeable. Therefore those that do in fact know something of the game have no tranquillity to work in peace. He believes in Saldanha as he has assisted the Brazilian players to win many games. His greatest virtue is the treatment of everyone on equal terms. He is a great friend of all the players firstly, and a manager, secondly. The worst thing, he says, is a player who does not trust his manager.

Tostão sleeps a lot, is calm and a keen observer. He is fond of detective fiction. All he owns (three apartments, a petrol station, a sports-goods store in Belo Horizonte, a beach house in Marataizes, and two cars) he obtained with his football career. He intends to become an economist when he is through with the game. He has three older brothers. One of them is an engineer.

Tostão is the quiet type who listens most of the time. He is a real perfectionist: when he began his career he neither kicked with his right nor ever tried to head the ball: he practised so much that nowadays he is extremely good at both. His personality is strong: he recently turned down a profitable publicity contract because it showed him in a different light.

He is in the process of acting out his own life in a film, as Pelé and Garrincha did before him. Tostão himself will narrate the film, expounding his thoughts, his joys, his sadnesses, on the outstanding facts and aspects of his life and career.

On one occasion he refused to obey an order given by manager Moreira to appear at a witchcraft session before a match against Santos in 1967. He also refused to carry a black chicken feather which would be released on entering the ground. None of which prevented him from playing an excellent game. From this point on superstition decreased in the Cruzeiro team.

Tostão has scored 250 goals in his career; he has been capped 35 times by his country and has scored the same number of goals (35) for the national side! He considers Saldanha the best manager he has ever had. Of the players he has seen, the best are Pelé, Bobby Charlton, Bobby Moore, Eusebio, and Florian Albert. He also likes Yashin, Perfumo, Rivera, Banks, Metrevelli and Rocha. Of the older generation he has great admiration for Di Stefano.

An exemplary athlete, highly disciplined, Tostão is very well liked by his colleagues. He loves football and feels that Brazil will never adopt brute-force Soccer, or play of a defensive nature. The art of the Brazilian player, an incomparable art, adapted to football where all ten players attack and defend, has turned the current Brazilian national side into the most complete football machine of all time.

Sir Alf Ramsey with the Jules Rimet Trophy, just before its journey to Mexico: 'England's current team' thinks Tostão, 'is better than the team which won the 1966 World Cup'.

GLAD I DIDN'T MISS

A FANTASTIC YEAR...

By DON ROGERS

(Swindon Town and England Under-23)

EVEN the most ingenious travel agent would be hard pressed to sell Swindon as a glamorous part of the country. Nor, for that matter, would the County Ground, eagerly waiting for the promised large-scale redevelopment to start, win any prizes in a competition for the most modern soccer stadiums.

Yet in the space of a few breathtaking months the name of Swindon Town Football Club echoed far and wide as the club enjoyed greater success and acclaim than many others have known in a lifetime.

Promotion to the Second Division, League Cup glory at Wembley, triumph in Europe, a good run in the FA Cup. This was the exciting, still almost unbelievable Swindon Soccer saga in 1969—a run of dramatic events, I will always remember in vivid detail, not least because I might easily have missed them all!

Not many Third Division clubs would have had the courage, let alone the faith to turn down a £100,000 offer for one of their players. This, I gather, was the sum they could easily have picked up for my services when several top-line First Division clubs obviously felt it would only be a matter of time

after our relegation to the Third Division in 1965, before I followed team-mates Ernie Hunt and Mike Summerbee into the First Division.

It is easy to understand why players become unsettled when their club is relegated, once you have suffered the experience yourself. I felt sick.

The bottom seemed to fall out of my football world for a while, although fortunately I soon realised, that as a 19-year-old at the time, there was time enough for me to make the grade again in years to come. Even so, relegation is something I never want to experience again. I wouldn't wish it on my worst enemy.

Twice while we were in the Third Division I asked for a transfer. We weren't doing too well at the time

97

and although I was scoring quite a few goals I just felt it was time for me to move.

It wasn't a question of wanting more money, it was mainly disillusionment. It wasn't made any easier by watching First Division matches on television and seeing players right in the limelight there, whom I knew were not really any better than myself.

Had the Swindon club granted my transfer request, I would definitely have moved on, despite the belief among some Pressmen that if it came to the crunch I would prefer to stay.

I admit I regard myself 100 per cent a Swindonian. It is my home town in every respect now but football's my life and if a move was necessary, it wouldn't bother me, wherever I went, providing I was playing football.

Equally, I am glad the Swindon directors took the stand they did in my case. I don't think I would ever have stopped kicking myself had I missed out on all the drama of a fantastic year.

Looking back, I might never have joined Swindon in the first place. For a while, when playing schoolboy football I was registered with Bristol City but they did not follow up their interest quickly enough and Bert Head, then manager of Swindon, and chief scout Ellis Stuttard stepped in.

I remember I signed for Swindon at 6 o'clock one evening and two hours later Fred Ford, then the Bristol City manager, was on the doorstep of my home in the Somerset village of Paulton with the invitation to make my career at Ashton Gate.

Joining a Football League club was a big step for me. I'd hardly been away from home, other than for holidays, before, but two years later I made the Football League team for the first time and luckily I've hardly looked back.

One of my greatest thrills was being nominated 'Player of the Tournament', as a member of the England Youth team which beat Spain to win the little World Cup. When I remind you that in the team were Peter Springett, Mick Wright, Bobby Noble, Howard Kendall, Alf Wood, John Hollins

Harry Redknap, Peter Knowles, and David Sadler, you will understand why I felt so honoured!

Since then I've made two appearances for the England Under-23 team and now my greatest ambition is to win a full England cap. The fact that we're back in the Second Division will, I hope, improve my chances in this respect, especially if I can continue to score goals as consistently as I did in the Third.

After all, Keith Newton seems to have settled happily into the England team while still a Second Division player with Blackburn Rovers. So why not me?

Managers, like players, differ of course from man to man. I've played under three at Swindon and all have helped me a great deal in their various ways, Bert Head probably most of all because he more or less taught me the way to play. When you leave school you think you can already play. In fact you're a long way from it.

Danny Williams was a fitness fanatic and quickly spotted that, although I don't actually dislike training, I sometimes need a bit of encouragement. Fred Ford is a different type again, down to earth but with a tremendous knowledge of the game and a great ability for making all his players believe in themselves.

Football to me is an art form, a way for the player to express himself. Scoring goals naturally gives me the greatest pleasure but equally I love to beat the full-back and lay the chance on for someone else.

People used to say I was a one-ground player, who would never turn it on away from home. Until a couple of seasons ago this was probably an accurate comment, but I have been disciplining myself to overcome that inhibition and now score almost as many goals away as I do at home.

I've changed my style and taken a freer role, largely to try and outwit those clubs who earmark one player to stay with me throughout the match. But clubs who do this are immediately reducing their own effective power to ten men, even if they succeed in shutting me out of the game.

A real West Country battle—Swindon's Thomas (dark shirt) about to be brought down by Bristol City's Parr. (Right) the spirit that took Swindon so far—Butler (dark shirt) defies Leeds' Norman Hunter and Gary Sprake.

IFB EDITORIAL

HIDDEN from the Western World, Communist China has a thriving Soccer organisation with several million players and attendances up to 100,000. For their own reasons the Chinese choose to remain aloof. This leaves only two major countries in the entire world where football of a high standard has yet to be developed. India and the United States of America.

As in so many other fields the Indians are held back by their outdated traditions and the multiplicity of religious problems, but the U.S.A. has no excuse. As far as Soccer is concerned the U.S.A. leading in almost every other facet of human endeavour, remains high on the list of undeveloped countries.

True the U.S.A. did beat England 1–0 in the 1950 World Cup and from time to time they have produced an equally-unexpected good result, but to the outsider the U.S.A. remains a non-starter. It is a fact, however, that though given little publicity Soccer has thrived at amateur level for a good many years, particularly in the states of New York and California; dominated in each case by European immigrants or the children of immigrants.

Given time and enthusiasm, Soccer is almost certain to catch on and when the snowball finally does begin to roll, it will skim off a great deal of the financial cream which is now cornered by the owners of the Baseball, American Football, Basketball, and Ice-Hockey teams.

Certainly an interest in Soccer exists and there are many parties who stand to benefit from its further development. Not least among this group are the small schools and colleges who find the costs of Soccer to be negligible when compared with providing for their students the elaborate and extremely expensive protective equipment which has become the standard in other U.S. games.

'The Americans, no less than the Russians, will not participate in anything unless they can count on being among the world's best' says IFB's Editorial: A Russian defender shows just what we mean, when out-climbing Northern Ireland's Derek Dougan . . .

Parents, too, are apparently satisfied to send their sons to Soccer-playing schools, for the American brand of football has an alarmingly high casualty rate. In one season in the '60s, more than 80 young men *died* as a result of injuries received whilst playing the American football game. By comparison the broken legs and arms, torn cartilages, and torn ankle ligaments which abound in Soccer are minor injuries.

Against this background it should not surprise anyone that throughout the United States more and more schools and colleges are switching from the American game to Soccer, and it is here that the most encouraging signs can be seen. American critics, however, have attempted to build up a case against Soccer, suggesting that it is in fact a game for 'cissies'—at one time believed to be a sure way of deterring the great American public.

The 1966 World Cup, televised across the U.S.A. in colour, convinced a great many people that Soccer was in fact no such thing. To the contrary it was seen to be a game of violence and physical contact and the decision was taken to introduce the European game to the U.S. public as a business venture.

Until then, big Soccer had invaded the U.S.A. only in the New York Tournaments staged in August each year, when a handful of good-class European and South American teams were invited to play just before their own seasons began. In effect the European teams that took part did no more than put on training sessions in the pre-season period and this was sold to the unsuspecting American fans as the real thing.

Later the big injection of money made an abortive attempt to produce Soccer in the U.S. on a grand scale. Owners of basketball and baseball teams were persuaded that their huge stadia, unused for three months of the year could be a financial proposition the year round.

That the grand experiment was to fail can be attributed to several different factors, varying from a lack of 'identity' between the imported players and the cities they played in; and the fact that a high proportion of the manager-coaches were only high-salaried 'conmen', while the bulk of the players were inevitably those who had failed to make the grade in their own country. In fact, a first-class game was packaged in a third-class wrapper.

In an attempt to offset their losses the 'owners' of the newly formed Soccer Clubs 'sold' television rights to nation-wide networks on terms that would make European fans spit. Indeed, when Soccer was televised in Britain on the commercial channels the TV Companies made the surpreme gaff by introducing unnatural breaks for advertising. Their switchboards must have been jammed for hours with enraged fans calling to point out that advertisements were acceptable *only* before the game; after the game; and at half-time. On this point there can be no compromise. Television must adapt itself to the game, for it cannot and will not, work the other way round.

Inevitably the television companies finally agreed that while the American public *might* 'buy' Soccer at international level it rejected the third-class players offered locally. When the TV companies withdrew their support it became clear that the entire undertaking was to be a costly failure and the businessmen pulled out. So too did the majority of players and coaches who were not so much dedicated to Soccer as seeking to make a living.

While a handful of Soccer faithfuls remained in the States, attempting to carry an enormous burden, the professional game neared its final collapse. Yet paradoxically at the same time Soccer has continued to gain more converts at high school and college level. The future therefore is almost assured, for when the youngsters of this decade, converted at school to Soccer, become the American citizens of tomorrow then Soccer will naturally and inevitably take its place among the other popular sports in the U.S.A.

'Thus Spake
Scaffold'

By THE SCAFFOLD, mostly ROGER McGOUGH

FOOTBALL? Why call it football? That's what you are probably saying to yourself. And you may well ask. Because it's fairly obvious that these days it should be called FEETball.

There are always 22 players on a pitch during any given game. They invariably have two feet each, as opposed to one foot between the lot of them, as the name of the game implies.

102

The Scaffold (left) in concert—Roger McGough (extreme right). An exciting 'Feetball' moment (right) as Middlesbrough's Hugh McIlmoyle challenges Manchester United's Ian Ure (white shirt) . . .

Remember that if they had three feet each, it could be comfortably re-named yardball. But that is nonsensical conjecture at this present time, at least as far as English teams are concerned.

And look at the sayings that surround the game. How often have you heard a jubilant commentator cry out with delight: 'See how light he is on his feet.' How foolish the poor man would feel if he was forced to burble 'See how light he is on his foot.'

Even in these days of the permissive society, equal rights for women, and drugs, it is a difficult problem. Imagine what might happen. . . .

. . . Feet on the march (or April, she's a nice girl —who's writing this, Roger?); banner-carrying bunions, 'Feet are Downtrodden'; 'Feet must stand up for their rights'; 'Dig your heels in'; 'Feet must put their foot down. . . .'

No, the situation is dangerous. It could get worse. But feet must be made to toe the line. And the organisation to do it will probably be the 'Society for the Correction of Catastrophes and Entertainment Reorganisation'.

SOCCER, as it will be known, will be set up soon after the year 2001 (for contractual reasons) to put sport firmly back where it belongs. Which is in show-business.

How much longer will fans stand for draughty accommodation, open to the worst vagaries of the English climate: rain, snow and even sun?

People will demand seats. Everybody will want to sit down to watch a match. And why not? How much longer will football club managements refuse to recognise that spectators have got joints?

And people will want to be able to book seats in advance just as they can for the theatre or the film-show. Why should supporters be penalised?

FEETball in the Year 2001

Clearly more thought has to be given to the public. And this will be yet another problem for SOCCER.

By the time SOCCER really starts, the game itself will have become much faster. So fast that it will take an entire team of officials aided by the latest electronic gadgetry to cope with each match. And as the working week gets shorter so fans will demand more games to watch.

Players will have to get much lighter in future. They will probably start getting much shorter as time goes on, so that they can move more quickly.

To keep up with the ever-increasing pace, four referees (or compères, as they will be known), four linesmen and a committee of judges will be required for each game. (This will help solve the inevitable unemployment problem in industry in the first years of the 21st century).

With so many people on the pitch, it will mean a whole new set of problems. For instance, the pitch will have to be divided into four quarters, with one compère in charge of each.

If an incident happened on the boundary of any of these quarters, it could easily result in a dispute between the referees. That's where the committee of judges comes in. They will be watching the match on television—with action replays every time there is a dispute.

And all the officials and extra technicians required will become employees of a Government Department attached to the Ministry of Entertainment (Sports Division).

It will also mean the end of the traditional mud and grass football pitch. It will become impossible to maintain them properly with so many matches being played each day, so clubs will have to instal synthetic pitches.

They will be impossible to wear out or down and the more progressive clubs will instal light beams running round the four sides which will set off a buzzer every time anything, or anyone, breaks the circuit.

Of course, the four Divisions will be broken up in favour of regionalised areas with each region maintaining about six teams. Consequently the dividends on the football pools will increase with a top prize of £5,000,000 each week.

There will be other problems, too. Liverpool will never be beaten after the Spring of 1994, so the Government may have to step in to force members of the team to move to other clubs.

But these are problems for our grandchildren to tackle. Our problem at the moment is forcing people to wake up to the fact that the game is misnamed.

We *know* it should be called FEETball. We play the game ourselves. And afterwards our feet make their own revolting protest about this ridiculous situation.

Look at the way your own feet react after a game. Weary, swollen, red with anger, their pride bruised and dented.

So drink-a-drink-a-drink with the Scaffold.

Join us in our great step forward for . . . FEET.

Arsenal's Bob McNab (right) clears a dangerous ball, leaving 'keeper Wilson and Sunderland's Kerr to sort themselves out.

The burly Eduard Streltzov, playing for Moscow Torpedo—the mystery man of Soviet Soccer . . .

THE Russian national team visited Britain in the autumn of 1945 stirring up a great deal of interest and proving, temporarily at least, that the Russians could play football. They came in disguise—labelled the Moscow Dynamo club—but whatever they called themselves there was no doubting their skill. In particular, the abilities of two of the inside-forward trio Bobrov and Beskov.

More than a decade was to pass before any other Russian team again ventured west of the Iron Curtain and when they did it was only to confirm that they too had embarked on the road that led away from the skilful game of the '30s, to the bustling, fighting brand of football we know today.

When the Russians did finally emerge from behind their wall it was to hammer Sweden 7-0 in Stockholm

VICTIM OR PRODUCT?

Strange and sad story
of Eduard Streltzov

and create a new image of invincibility. Though not another Bobrov, the young centre-forward Eduard Streltzov, scorer of a hat-trick in this match—his début in the national team—was one of the few Russian players to cause any real excitement.

Skilful, intelligent, and quick, Streltzov preferred the delicate flick of a first-time pass, or a body feint, to send an opponent the wrong way while he turned. For the rest, one Russian player is like another—

By ERIC BATTY

they play as if they had been produced in some Siberian factory: strong, speedy, determined, disciplined, methodical. But dull.

There have been exceptions—Sergei Salnikov was certainly talented; Igor Chislenko was, on his day, among the best wingers in the world; and of the present generation Anatoli Bychevecz and Vladimir Mountian might well develop into world-class players. But the big exception of the '50s was Eduard Streltzov: and he spent the best years of his football-life in prison.

At 16, Streltzov was unknown except amongst his workmates at the garage where he worked as an apprentice mechanic until his talent was spotted by an official of the Torpedo Moscow club. Streltzov signed for Torpedo—the sports club of Faline, the car-manufacturing company. In a matter of months Streltzov had established himself in the first XI and at 17 he got his first cap.

At 18 he starred in the 1956 Olympics squad which won the football Gold Medals and a year later, despite his talents on the field, he was suspended for two months for his conduct off it. Streltzov's Torpedo club-mate Valentin Ivanov was suspended with him . . . for drinking and failing to set an example to the youth of the nation.

Ivanov was to see the wisdom of mending his ways and later became manager of his old club after gaining more than 50 caps, while Streltzov was to stray too far. At 19, Streltzov was back at his best to regain his place in the national team and at 20 he was given Russia's supreme award . . . Footballer of the Year. *Then, suddenly, the roof fell in.*

A wild and drunken party led to a young girl being accidentally killed when she fell down a flight of stairs. Later, she was found to be pregnant, and Streltzov's career lay in ruins. Twenty-one years old, with 13 full caps to his credit, Streltzov was sentenced to 12 years hard labour.

A 'model' prisoner, Streltzov received the maximum remission of one-half of the sentence and was released in 1964. At 27, he began to play again in Torpedo's reserve team. A year later in 1965, Streltzov was granted FA permission to play again in the League side.

The leading Russian goal-scorer that season, he played a vital role in Torpedo's Championship success and later won two FA Cup Winners' medals in successive years. But in 1965, when the FA were finally persuaded to allow Streltzov to play in the first team, it was a condition that he must not play for the national team and must never be allowed to play abroad.

Before the 1966 World Cup it was common knowledge that national selector-coach Nikolai Morosov had repeatedly asked the FA for permission to bring back Streltzov. 'Without him', said Morosov, 'we cannot win, we have no one else who can play the centre-forward game as he can.'

Nineteen-sixty-seven was a big year for Streltzov, not only successful but giving a hint of what he might have become but for those lost six years. For Eduard, now 30 years old, the wheel was to turn full circle. First he scored his 100th League goal to join a very select band of only 12 men to reach three figures before him; was given once more the title 'Honoured Master of Sport', and after producing a fine game against England at Wembley in the 2-2 draw of December, 1967, he was proclaimed once more— 'Footballer of the Year'.

Streltzov was not by any means the only person convicted in court for offences connected with alcohol—and not even the only well-known footballer. While Streltzov served his sentence, another Moscow international, Juri Sevidov of Spartak, was sentenced to ten years gaol after killing a pedestrian whilst driving under the influence of drink. More recently a prospective member of Russia's 1970 World Cup squad—Anatoli Banischewski (Neftchki-Baku)—was suspended for two years for conduct (drinking) which was incompatible with the life of a sportsman.

Throughout 1968 Streltzov apparently devoted himself to training and playing, but the new World Cup squad boss, Gavril Katchalin, had no place for one who would be 33 in Mexico. 1969 began brightly, too, with Streltzov gaining a place in the Russian FA's New Year's Honours list as the best centre-forward.

But before the year was out, Streltzov had been suspended for one month (by the FA) after arguing with a referee; temporarily suspended and ordered not to attend the Torpedo ground for training; and finally barred from the club for life . . . for conduct unbecoming a sportsman.

Again the wheel has turned for Streltzov. He is back where he started—a mechanic in the Faline factory, who, it is said, was a good player in his day. Yet, in the west, we still know very little of Streltzov the man; his motives, what precisely made him tick.

Does the Soviet system of well-paid amateurism produce bored young men with nothing to do most of the time—except to drink and get in trouble? Or does the system, by wooing the outstanding sportsmen and women, cosmonauts and scientists, use the few who fall by the wayside as examples in their propaganda campaign to keep the nation's young people away from the 'devil drink'.

Recognising that we shall never know the man himself, we will never know whether Eduard Streltzov was a product of the Soviet system . . . or one of its victims.

A Prime Minister relaxes . . . and his guest at a party at No. 10 Downing Street is Manchester United's George Best. Mr Wilson's party was in honour of the West German Chancellor, Herr Willy Brandt.

TBALL SWORD OF HONOUR 1970

'For distinguished service to British and international football'

LAWS OF THE GAME PERFECTLY CLEAR

BY SIR STANLEY ROUS, C.B.E., J.P.
President of F.I.F.A.

WORLD Cup Year. Those three simple words dominated football in 1970, and brought us yet again to the culmination, this time in Mexico in summer, of one of the world's most extraordinary sporting events—the World Football Championship for the Jules Rimet Trophy. Sixteen nations contested the Final competition, the glamour of which often makes us forget that those 16

Not quite there!—Manchester City's Neil Young reaches to tackle United's Willy Morgan, but Morgan's shot beats him. Ian St John (right), seen from a 45-degree angle!—the Liverpool forward is up to beat Wolves' back Parkin . . .

teams emerged from a qualifying competition which was spread over two years; which involved more than 100 of the Soccer-playing nations of the world, and which meant a programme of qualifying matches in virtually every country in the world. And it also brings to a climax six years of planning by FIFA, the world governing body, and their Mexican hosts— the football association, the government and indeed the people of this remarkable Central American republic.

For those of us involved in football at any rate, the World Cup is the greatest show on earth, holding the attention through the world's Press and television media, of hundreds of millions of people intent on thrilling action from outstanding players in teams engaged in competitive action of the highest order. All this is hugely glamorous, yet it tends to obscure

Southampton's Terry Paine slips a tackle from a West Ham defender.

he massive background to the event, one which nvolves enormous planning.

One of the most critical factors in planning is the venue of the final tournament. Why Mexico? The venue for the 1970 competition was decided in 1964, at the Tokyo Congress of FIFA, held during the Olympic Games of that year. Mexico won by a large majority over Argentina, the other nation applying for the Championships. Historically, the first World Cup final competition was played in Uruguay in 1930. Two more followed in Europe, in France and Italy, in 1934 and 1938. After the war, Brazil was host in 1950, then Switzerland in 1954, Sweden in 1958.

The pattern was emerging—twice in Europe, once in South America, reflecting the power of football geographically in the world. In 1962, the Finals were in Chile, in 1966 in England. The advent of jet-air travel at the end of the '50s made it possible to stage the Championship more easily almost anywhere in the world—at least from the point of view of travel—and there is every reason, to suppose that, in time the Final competition will be staged in Africa or Asia.

FIFA has the sole right to organise the World Championships, its Executive Committee the sole right of selecting venues. The regulations now demand that Championships must be staged successively in different continents (this reflecting the spreading power of the world-wide game) and the host country must give to the Executive Committee certain assurances—financial assurances, a guarantee of facilities and conditions, a guarantee of entry visas to all participants, and so on.

The increasing strength and attraction of the game and the competition soon made it clear that inter-

Soccer—sunshine style: Atletico de Madrid centre-forward Luis leaps over Las Palmas' 'keeper Ulacia.

Who'd have the goalkeeper's life?—above: it's Calvin Palmer (as substitute) trying to smother a shot from Stoke winger Mahoney; below: it's Burnley 'keeper Mellor making a fine save from Liverpool's Graham.

ested countries were making excessive efforts to influence the Executive Committee. Thousands of pounds were being spent on presentations and hospitality and propaganda, and downright lobbying. I felt that this was unnecessary, and slightly distasteful and fortunately the Executive Committee agreed to a proposal from me that the committee should select venues in advance to avoid all this. Thus the following timetable was adopted:

1970	Mexico
1974	West Germany (Spain withdrew a strong application)
1978	Argentina
1982	Spain

Yugoslavia and the United States of America have already made tentative approaches for 1986!

In the past ten years, the Mexicans have been remarkably active in presenting major international sport and have acquired a very wide experience of it, in world amateur and professional golf, Pan-American Games, and finally in 1968, the Olympic Games themselves. We have every confidence that the organisation will be excellent and fully up to the required FIFA standards.

Of course, the one outstanding doubt about Mexico as a sporting venue has been altitude. We have concluded that this should present no great problem for footballers and referees who are properly acclimatised, since they have the opportunity for 'rest' within the game itself, and are not continuously expending energy for the entire 90 minutes, as marathon and distance runners must do in a very concentrated manner.

There is a good deal more to World Championships than bands and waving flags, players, and huge stadia. Referees are of critical importance, particularly at a stage in the history of the game in which the rewards can be enormously high for professional players and in which the competitive element is becoming more and more pronounced. This in turn puts heavy pressure on referees who are virtually

Where's it gone?—Leicester 'keeper Shilton must be wondering about that ball, having been beaten by Southampton's Ron Davies.

volunteers, and amateurs. Not yet do we have full-time professional referees, and I am not sure that we ever shall, and match fees just cannot be related to the responsibility a man bears when he is refereeing, for example, a World Cup final before 105,000 people, as one man certainly did on June 21, 1970, in Mexico City's stunning Azteca Stadium.

In addition, referees have this problem of varying interpretations of the Laws of the Game, or more accurately, varying *applications* of the Laws of the Game. This is FIFA's constant concern. We all know that historically, and from habit, different countries, or different regions of the world, actually play the game in slightly different ways. This is a generalisation of course, but it is not inaccurate to say that the British and Northern European countries accept strong physical challenge and direct frontal tackling as intrinsic within the spirit of the game, and of course clearly permitted in the Laws. On the other hand, the Latins and South Americans dislike this, dispense with it to a large degree, but on the other hand are much more addicted to obstructive football. Yet we in FIFA are content that the Laws of the Game are in turn perfectly clear on what is and is not permissible. We sought to impress this on the referees in Mexico.

The 30 referees appointed to the Final Competition were 'inspected' all through the preliminary matches. They were invited to Mexico in ample time for a proper acclimatisation, for pre-Championship training and briefing, and for a detailed programme which helped ensure a more uniform application of laws. This has been done successfully at all FIFA tournaments, at Olympic Games, and World Championships for several years. There were a higher percentage of referees from neutral countries—countries which did not have competing teams—than ever before, with 18 of them, nine from participating countries, and three from Mexico.

Communication and language is always a big problem in these international gatherings. We hoped to ease it by having the referees form teams of three,

Hat-trick for Peter 'Ossie' Osgood of Chelsea, against Sunderland—and here's the first.

Liverpool's Geoff Strong flicks this ball over Coventry 'keeper Glazier to score. Newcastle's Ian McFall (below) makes sure of this save from Spurs' Martin Chivers.

Chelsea defenders David Webb and John Hollins (right) can't contain flying John Hindley of Nottingham Forest as he forces the ball away between them . . .

each team having at least one common language. In addition, we used the disc system of communicating with players. Each referee had a yellow disc, which meant that the player was being cautioned, and a red disc which meant he was being ordered to leave the field. The 1968 Olympic Games saw this system started with much success and it was done in Mexico again, this year. Two substitutes were allowed at any time during each match. Referees had a list of eleven starting players, plus another group of five, from which the two substitutes could be drawn.

Again a Technical Study Committee, directed by Walter Winterbottom and assisted by Ron Greenwood of England; Dettmar Cramer of West Ger-

Playing at Polar bears?—no, it's a very serious business as Liverpool's Ian St John gets this ball away in a swirl of snow from Nottingham Forest's Joe Baker.

many, our FIFA coach, and Sandro Puppol of Italy, reported to the FIFA Technical Committee on the preparation, training, tactics, skills, and formations of the teams in the championship, and on referees. Harry Cavan of Northern Ireland is chairman of that committee.

We at FIFA had no intention of teaching referees the Laws of the Game for the World Cup. They already knew them, just as all players should know them. Rather we tried to effect a uniform application of these laws and we used films, slides, lectures, and discussions to help achieve this.

Unlike many, I am not convinced that there are 'easy' groups and 'difficult' groups in these Finals.

Football becomes more and more even between the nations of the world every year. I subscribe to the belief that if any team is to earn the proud title 'World Champions', it must be prepared to face and defeat any other team in the world, regardless of the luck of the draw.

Some old friends were missing—Austria, Scotland, Argentina, Portugal, Yugoslavia. On the other hand, as ever, there were new faces—El Salvador, Rumania, Peru, Israel, Morocco. It is this constant tide of change which adds so much flavour to the competition. Marvellously talented players and thrilling teams took part, and it is my hope that whether you were in Mexico, or followed the action on television, you saw outstanding matches played in a mature and honourable sporting spirit.

Stanley Rous

Derby's Kevin Hector looks confident about this one, but that ball was picked up by Forest 'keeper Hill . . .

'If there was football

on the moon Sir Stanley

would be an astronaut'

EXCALIBUR: the sword of Damocles. How symbolic is the shining blade in mythology. And now there is the Sword of Honour, this year delivered to the trusty right hand of Sir Stanley Rous for his immeasurable services to football. Sword on one side; like justice itself he bears also, unseen, the scales of justice.

Following in the footsteps of Sir Matt Busby, Sir Stanley Matthews, Pelé, Jock Stein, the late Willy Meisl and Bobby Charlton, all of whom variously distinguished themselves in the cause of this universal game, Sir Stanley now becomes the first senior administrator to be thus honoured.

FOOTBALL SWORD
OF HONOUR 1970
SIR
STANLEY ROUS, C.B.E.

There could scarcely be a worthier choice. But where, one would wonder, is this finely-turned prize

By GEOFFREY GREEN
Association Football
Correspondent of *The Times*

to be found room-space in a home already bulging at the seams with honours and gifts gathered in from the four corners of the globe? Sir Stanley is the father figure and respected head of a family that knows no bounds.

It was in the winter of 1949 that I wrote a 'Sporting Print' of him in *The Observer* at a time when, as the paid Secretary of the Football Association, he had his guiding hand on the tiller of that historic ship. If I may be forgiven repetition, these were the opening two paragraphs:

'In a quiet square off Lancaster Gate there stands a monument. Within a stone's throw of it is the office and home of Sir Stanley Rous. There would seem to be a curious symbolism in their juxtaposition.

'It is a four-sided monument, simple and unadorned. On each of its sides are engraved the words "North—South—East—West". At its pinnacle sits the figure of a young boy: at its base the inscription,

Glyn Pardoe scores Manchester City's winning goal against West Bromwich Albion in the League Cup Final at Wembley.

"Youth and Empire". For Sir Stanley that monument would be complete with the addition of two words: "Youth and Empire—*and World*".'

Destiny has brought that to pass. Elected President of the Federation Internationale de Football Association (FIFA) in 1961, for all but ten years now he has stood at the pinnacle of world football, the very apex of the vast pyramid whose broad base represent the youth of every nation of whatever colour or creed, who live under many skies..

Yet basically it is one sky, one game, and it is this universality that Sir Stanley has always fought to maintain in a world of many voices and many tongues, where rival schisms have constantly threatened disruption. It is a massive Tower of Babel

and to bring some measure of order and coherence to it has required the wisdom of a Solomon.

It is an endless, often thankless duty, demanding almost ceaseless travel from one continent to another across the windy roof of the world. Many a young man's strength would long ago have been sapped by the mere physical requirements of the task, to say nothing of the myriad problems that walk hand in hand with it all. But not this hardy warrior, who survives because fundamentally he remains young at heart. Were football played on the moon there is no doubt that Sir Stanley would long since have become an astronaut.

Rather, a diplomat by instinct, he has become the ambassador of sport, walking the corridors of power yet uncorrupted by it. If he does not suffer fools glady it is because his day is not long enough. So much to do: so little time to do it. But the honest man will always find a sympathetic ear whatever the pressures of an instant world where so many are forced to run before they can even walk straight.

Since leaving his position as games master at Watford Grammar School in 1933—at a time when he was also a member of the Hertfordshire FA

Council—he has found the ascending escalator of life. Succeeding Sir Frederick Wall as Secretary of the FA in 1934, he held that important post for a quarter of a century while the rigid conventions of an earlier age were quietly disturbed.

Sir Stanley's hand was to be detected in many of those revolutionary changes—the appointment of Walter Winterbottom as first FA Director of Coaching and as England's team manager; the return of

the British Associations to the fold of FIFA after the second World War; the interchange of British and foreign referees; a Provident Fund for professional players; the extension of international youth tournaments.

Beyond all this, too, time somehow was found to touch on local government, be a member on the Organising Committees of the past six Olympiads; serve on the Executive Committee of the King George Jubilee Trust, be closely connected with the Central Council of Physical Recreation, and help even in the expansion of the National Association of Boys' Clubs. The list is endless. In a single span Sir Stanley has lived the lives of many men.

Unlike one who resides in a valley, influenced by the shadows of a valley, Sir Stanley lives at the mountain top. His views are wide and all-embracing; his horizons limitless. Football is his game and the world his playing pitch. As becomes one who refereed the Cup Final of 1934, he still remains a referee in a wider context, ever watchful of trends, and seeing to it that the Laws of the Game—which he helped to rewrite in 1938—are followed by the amateur and the professional wherever they may be.

To touch perhaps on one of the ruling passions of his full life is to touch on a desire to help in the physical and mental uplifting of young people everywhere; to give youth, in fact, the opportunity to play the game, in its every sense, north—south—east—and west.

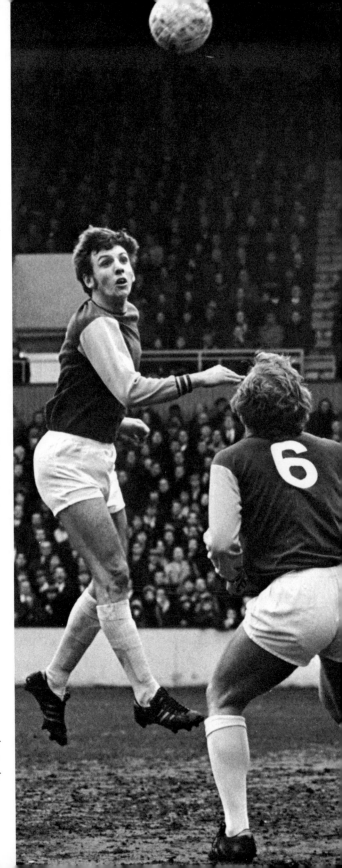

Nottingham Forest's Peter Hindley shows how to keep your eye on that ball as he races Derby's O'Hare for it; right: a fine shot of Martin Peters (now with Spurs) and former West Ham colleague Bobby Moore.

THE BEST ENGLAND TEAM OF MY TIME

BY JIMMY GREAVES
(West Ham and England)

WHEN I look back to the time when I started playing for England—and it's a long look back because my first full representative games were in 1959—memories flood back of a great many brilliant players. World-beaters, most of them, and it was a privilege to be part of all those different combinations of talent.

But there were so many of them. One question I'm asked frequently is: 'What would be the line-up of your *best* England eleven?' and it's a very tricky problem to solve. How can you separate so many top-class players, bridging the best part of a decade of Soccer? Still, a serious question deserves a serious answer, so I settled down to pick out the absolute cream from a tremendously talented list of players.

Maybe one or two of my selections will surprise you. Maybe you'll get upset at some of the omissions. But that, as they say, is football! One thing: I was urged to include myself in the side, wearing the number eight shirt, but I've decided to avoid that. I've picked a side of my all-time greats, but reserved a seat in the front of the stand for myself.

Now when it comes to goal-keeping, the problem isn't so tough. I go immediately to Gordon Banks, once Leicester and now Stoke City—and I go to him with the green jersey simply because he is the best 'keeper in the world. I've seen most of the others, all over the world, but nobody can keep 'Banksie' out of the top place.

When they were rivals . . . Jimmy Greaves appears to be tripping West Ham's Bobby Moore. Later in the season, Greaves joined West Ham . . . and Moore won't be unhappy about that!

His anticipation is magnificent—he senses danger where many other international 'keepers are simply guessing. He cuts out the high cross with brilliant skill. He has agility. If most of us have five senses, he seems to have seven. What is more, he is tremendously consistent. Maybe there are more showy keepers, but Gordon Banks is the complete professional—creating his own brand of miracle-making.

In the right-back slot comes Jimmy Armfield, that fine one-club man from Blackpool. He was the original overlapping full-back, making ground by his sheer speed and he added that extra touch of excitement to England performances in the early '60s. Of course, George Cohen carried on the knack of haring up-field, but Jimmy Armfield was the first, and he's certainly my first choice in this position.

As a partner, I couldn't do better than pick Ray Wilson. Now here is a Mr Consistency of England football—I don't suppose anybody was more consistent than Ray, except, perhaps, Bobby Moore. Ray was something of a rarity, a Second Division clubman with Huddersfield Town, before moving to Everton; but he was certainly a player of tremendous class.

So now we go to the number four shirt. Here I'll pick Nobby Stiles, the Manchester United terrier. Point is that he is a great 90-minute player and also consistent. From the front, we can look over our shoulders and be sure that he's doing his job rather better than most. But there is also the fact that he can mix it a bit, and I think every team should have a player of that type. Nobby is one of those great-hearted players who also has a great deal of talent.

At centre-half: Jackie Charlton, of Leeds United. Not only is he a great centre-half, defensively, he is also so strong in going forward at the right moment and scoring an all-important goal. This kind of versatility in a 'big fella' is a valuable asset to any team as he's certainly proved many times while in the England side.

In the number six position, I simply have to pick Bobby Moore. As far as I'm concerned, he is the best defender in the world—bar none. There really is

little more I can say about the West Ham reliable, except that he is also a first-rate skipper, constantly urging his men on. But if you're the best, then you're the best. No point arguing further!

On the right-wing, maybe a surprise selection. I'd go for Bryan Douglas, formerly with Blackburn Rovers and now, as far as I know, with Great Harwood in the Northern Premier League. Bryan gets his place, despite some very strong opposition, because he is a terrific man at working the ball. He turns on his skills in the tightest of positions and this is another most valuable asset to the side. I firmly believe that he'd be an England regular now, if only the passing years hadn't taken their toll.

Number eight and it's certainly not me. It's Francis Lee, of Manchester City. In a sense, he and I play the same way, running through the defence, but he's got a terrific amount of energy and style and wastes no time in having a bang at goal. Besides,

he'd be a perfect decoy for my choice to wear the number nine shirt.

Which is Bobby Smith, my old team-mate at Tottenham. Bobby, a battering-ram of a centre-forward, put the fear of death into everyone who faced him. But it's a mistake to think that he was just a battering-ram. Bobby had a lot of skill to go with his determination to turn any half-chance into a goal and he was a tremendous spearhead of the England attack for part of the time I was in the side.

So now it's inside-left. And Johnny Haynes—who else? I don't think there has been a better mid-field player since the war, never mind just the years I was in the team. A brilliant split-second passer of the ball, the Fulham man could control his own part of the field with superlative skill. So he's a natural for my own England team.

Only one to go now, and in comes Bobby Charlton, of Manchester United. Wearing the number 11 shirt? Yes, because that's the position he held originally in the England side. He could be relied upon to beat his man going down the line, and then get over a precision cross. A fine all-round player, of course. Maybe he still *could* take on the best in the world on that touch-line, but his role for England has clearly changed with the new systems employed.

Incidentally I picked Francis Lee instead of Geoff Hurst simply because I think he'd play rather better with Smith.

Well, there it is—11 players selected from the many I had the honour of playing with in the England white shirt. I gave it a great deal of thought. My view is that this team could line-up 4–2–4 formation, with Johnny Haynes and Nobby Stiles in midfield.

Or, if required, it would do just as well in the 4-3-3 system, with Bryan Douglas held back for midfield.

But I did warn you that you wouldn't agree with all my selections. Still, part of the interest in football is in holding a post-mortem on what happened and what might have been.

The first of that mammoth series of United-Leeds Cup Semi-Finals . . . Jackie Charlton and Mick Jones of Leeds and United's Ian Ure show (left) just how tough those ties were, before Leeds emerged victors from the third of them. Right: anything goes!—a tussle featuring Derby 'keeper Les Green plus Joe Royle of Everton and a brace of Derby defenders.

I'M NO 'FRANKENSTEIN'

BY JOE ROYLE
of Everton

EVERTON'S superb training headquarters at Bellefield on the outskirts of Liverpool has earned the reputation of being one of the classiest, most productive training centres in Soccer throughout the world.

But some of the stories I've heard about my own training sessions at Bellefield would give you the impression that it's a dark, secret place where 'professor' Harry Catterick has been busy secretly assembling a manufactured, patented Soccer player.

It has become a favourite word in Soccer—a

'manufactured' player—ever since Manchester City's chief coach Malcolm Allison began describing goalkeeper Joe Corrigan in such a way. He reasoned that Corrigan had not been a natural goalkeeper but, with plenty of hard work and patience, has been instilled with some sort of artificial instinct for the job.

People conjured up ideas of Allison in some dark laboratory creating a goalkeeper out of thin air. They did not realise that a player has to have the raw materials in terms of basic skill and expertise to suit him to the job.

Anyway, when stories began to reach the newspapers about me returning to Bellefield after normal training, and in the close season, for special training

The 'devil' and Joe Royle—the special 'bite' which gives Joe his reputation; it's Forest 'keeper Hill (top) just pipping the Everton leader to a high one; it's Royle again—this time dividing Hill (left) from Forest team-mate Hindley . . .

schedules they began to wonder if I, too, was a 'manufactured' player; somebody who was not a natural footballer but who had to be taken to pieces and reassembled as a player who could apply his heading ability to making and taking goals.

Well, I can tell them that this is not so. What is true is that I am a late developer who had to make up for lost time.

I began my career at school as a defender and I always regarded myself in that light until I was seen by Mr Catterick who instantly thought that I would make a better attacker than defender. In fact, in all my time at Everton I have only once played wing-half, when one of the junior teams was short of defenders and well off for attackers.

But for the rest of the time Everton have seen me purely and simply as an attacker and that is the role I am best suited to. All those 'secret' training sessions with Mr Catterick and the Everton training staff were not to create a player but to tone up the one they already had.

There is much more to playing centre-forward than people imagine and like any trade this one has its short-cuts and little 'fiddles'. You must learn the techniques and apply them in the right place at the right time and my long spells of 'overtime' were spent learning those.

It's not so much a matter of timing because I don't believe this is something you can be taught—it has to come naturally or you will never have it—but a question of where to go, what to do, in given situations. These are not things that necessarily come naturally but have to be taught in situations artificially created.

It's obvious that a dentist is not going to practise drawing and filling teeth on real people, but on dummies, before going on to real people in the Dental hospital. It's very much the same in a situation like mine where, because I was a late developer as a striker, I had to learn to react to real situations in an artificially-created environment before putting them into effect in full-scale practice matches.

I might now have a reputation for being able to head a ball, but this didn't come naturally to me. This was something that Mr Catterick worked on until I was able to head a ball with varying degrees

of power and accuracy, given ever-changing situations. In schoolboy football I never had to jump for a ball because I was taller than the rest of the lads, and I had to work on this.

Even jumping for the ball with the opposing centre-half requires different techniques. Sometimes you have to get up earlier than the centre-half, 'hovering' for a split-second before the ball arrives, which is all a question of timing. Some centre-halves jump with you—usually the best centre-halves do this—while others, less confident, less assured, jump at you to try to shift you bodily away from the line and flight of the ball.

Now that I have had something like three years experience in the First Division—I made my début at the ripe old age of 16 against Blackpool in January 1966—I have learned how to assess the different approaches of centre-halves. I have played against every centre-half in the First Division, apart from those from the promoted clubs of course, at least four times and that of course is enough to know which approach each favours.

For sheer effectiveness Ron Yeats of our old rivals Liverpool is the best centre-half I have played against because he does the job his club wants him to do . . . act as a solid stopper down the middle of the park. Mike England is a good centre-half, but I have less trouble with him since I learned how to apply myself physically to my game.

As I say, I've played against every First Division centre-half, but there are a lot of good centre-halves throughout Europe I have yet to meet up with. Everton have had plenty of success over the years but since the time I came into the team we have not been in European competition—until this next season. Although I have played in some international games at Under-23 level I've never competed in international club competitions which I'm really looking forward to.

This was something I had dreamed about when I

Joe Royle (below) slides in desperately, but Forest's Hill and Hennessey come out winning; Royle takes off superbly (top, right), to get one past Derby's Dave Mackay; another fine Royle header (below, right)— saved this time by Leeds' Gary Sprake.

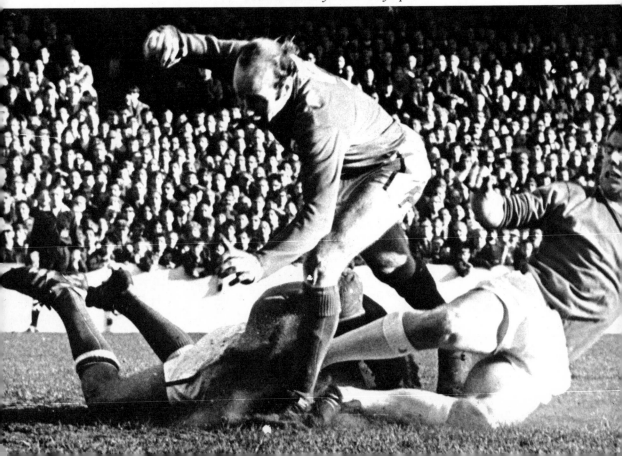

was told on that January day four years ago that I was in the team. I said at the time when I first heard the news: 'I have always dreamed about turning out for the first team but I never expected it so soon. I am feeling a bit nervous now but I hope to have got over the shock in time for tomorrow's match. It will be a great feeling putting on a first team jersey.'

Let me tell you that that feeling has never left me. I still feel the same way whenever I pull on the Everton shirt which up to the end of last season (1969–70) I had done something like 122 times in League matches with over 60 goals in that time.

I feel that although I am still only 20 years old I have matured under the guidance of Mr Catterick but I still have to look at myself in the mirror every now and again to reassure myself that, in spite of what some people say, I am not Harry Catterick's 'Frankenstein Monster'. Just a lad who wanted to play football and who went to the best club in the country to make him realise his full potential. I owe Everton something for that, for having faith in me, and the best way I can repay them is by scoring goals.

I hope to keep repaying them in this way until the end of my playing career. They not only made me into a better player than I may have been had I gone to another club but here at Everton I have found myself playing with the best midfield trio in Soccer —Colin Harvey, Howard Kendall, and Alan Ball.

For a centre-forward, playing in front of players like this is almost like playing snooker with someone who keeps leaving the black ball on the lip of the pocket for you!

A look of pain on Manchester United's Willy Morgan's face as he comes crashing down after a tackle by Leed's Terry Cooper.

THE YEAR'S INTERNATIONAL FOOTBALL

There is space for only the minimum of explanatory text to this year's statistical pages that must include the completion of the results of the various group competitions for the 1970 World Championship. The final matches themselves will have been played in Mexico by the time this annual is in your hands but for those readers who like to maintain their records in the successive IFB annuals, the final page has been set aside for them to complete the details of the Mexican matches. The line-ups for the more important national teams in their 1970 World Championship matches will be featured, of course, in next year's IFB in these end pages. For the moment, apart from the usual interest in this record of line-ups, many readers will probably find it instructive to compare the recorded 1969 line-ups of countries as, for examples, Brazil, Italy, the Soviet Union, West Germany—and England, with those that took the field for the World Championship matches in Mexico. Finally, for the benefit of any readers new to IFB this year, I should explain that, as last year for that matter, I have tried to make a tentative departure from the traditional positional references and to show some line-ups in 4-2-4 or 4-3-3 formation but even when so doing I am conscious that the fluidity of play makes any positional notation no more than a rough approximation of the role played by a particular player.

GORDON JEFFERY

WORLD CHAMPIONSHIP—JULES RIMET CUP 1970

THE QUALIFYING COMPETITION (Outstanding results from March 1969)

Group 1

Greece	2	Rumania	2
Portugal	0	Switzerland	2
Portugal	2	Greece	2
Switzerland	0	Rumania	1
Rumania	1	Portugal	0
Greece	4	Switzerland	1
Switzerland	1	Portugal	1
Rumania	1	Greece	1

	P	W	D	L	F	A	Pts
Rumania	6	3	2	1	7	6	8
Greece	6	2	3	1	13	9	7
Switzerland	6	2	1	3	5	8	5
Portugal	6	1	2	3	8	10	4

Group 2

Rep. of Ireland	1	Czechoslovakia	2
Hungary	2	Czechoslovakia	0
Denmark	2	Rep. of Ireland	0
Rep. of Ireland	1	Hungary	2
Denmark	3	Hungary	2
Czechoslovakia	3	Hungary	3
Czechoslovakia	3	Rep. of Ireland	0
Rep. of Ireland	1	Denmark	1
Hungary	3	Denmark	0
Hungary	4	Rep. of Ireland	0

	P	W	D	L	F	A	Pts
Czechoslovakia	6	4	1	1	12	6	9
Hungary	6	4	1	1	16	7	9
Denmark	6	2	1	3	6	10	5
Rep. of Ireland	6	0	1	5	3	14	1

Play-off:

Czechoslovakia	4	Hungary	1

Group 3

E. Germany	2	Italy	2
E. Germany	2	Wales	1
Wales	1	E. Germany	3
Italy	4	Wales	1
Italy	3	E. Germany	0

	P	W	D	L	F	A	Pts
Italy	4	3	1	0	10	3	7
E. Germany	4	2	1	1	7	7	5
Wales	4	0	0	4	3	10	0

Group 4

N. Ireland	0	U.S.S.R.	0
U.S.S.R.	3	Turkey	0
U.S.S.R.	2	N. Ireland	0
Turkey	1	U.S.S.R.	3

	P	W	D	L	F	A	Pts
U.S.S.R.	4	3	1	0	8	1	7
N. Ireland	4	2	1	1	7	3	5
Turkey	4	0	0	4	2	13	0

Group 5

Norway	2	Sweden	5
Norway	1	France	3
Sweden	2	France	0
France	3	Sweden	0

	P	W	D	L	F	A	Pts
Sweden	4	3	0	1	12	5	6
France	4	2	0	2	6	6	4
Norway	4	1	0	3	4	13	2

Group 6

Spain	2	Yugoslavia	1
Finland	1	Yugoslavia	5
Finland	2	Spain	0
Spain	6	Finland	0
Yugoslavia	4	Belgium	0

	P	W	D	L	F	A	Pts
Belgium	6	4	1	1	14	8	9
Yugoslavia	6	3	1	2	19	7	7
Spain	6	2	2	2	10	6	6
Finland	6	1	0	5	6	28	2

Group 7

Scotland	1	W. Germany	1
Cyprus	1	Austria	2
W. Germany	1	Austria	0
Scotland	8	Cyprus	0
W. Germany	12	Cyprus	0
W. Germany	3	Scotland	2
Austria	2	Scotland	0

	P	W	D	L	F	A	Pts
W. Germany	6	5	1	0	20	3	11
Scotland	6	3	1	2	18	7	7
Austria	6	3	0	3	12	7	6
Cyprus	6	0	0	6	2	35	0

Group 8

Poland	8	Luxembourg	1
Bulgaria	2	Luxembourg	1
Netherlands	1	Poland	0
Bulgaria	4	Poland	1
Poland	2	Netherlands	1
Luxembourg	1	Poland	5
Netherlands	1	Bulgaria	1
Poland	3	Bulgaria	0
Luxembourg	1	Bulgaria	3

	P	W	D	L	F	A	Pts
Bulgaria	6	4	1	1	12	7	9
Poland	6	4	0	2	19	8	8
Netherlands	6	3	1	2	9	5	7
Luxembourg	6	0	0	6	4	24	0

Group 9 ENGLAND qualified as the title-holders

Group 10

Bolivia	3	Argentina	1
Peru	1	Argentina	0
Bolivia	2	Peru	1
Peru	3	Bolivia	0
Argentina	1	Bolivia	0
Argentina	2	Peru	2

	P	W	D	L	F	A	Pts
Peru	4	2	1	1	7	4	5
Bolivia	4	2	0	2	5	6	4
Argentina	4	1	1	2	4	6	3

Group 11

Colombia	3	Venezuela	0
Venezuela	1	Colombia	1
Colombia	0	Brazil	2
Venezuela	0	Paraguay	2
Venezuela	0	Brazil	5
Colombia	0	Paraguay	0
Paraguay	0	Brazil	3
Paraguay	1	Venezuela	0
Brazil	6	Colombia	0
Paraguay	2	Colombia	1
Brazil	6	Venezuela	0
Brazil	1	Paraguay	0

	P	W	D	L	F	A	Pts
Brazil	6	6	0	0	23	2	12
Paraguay	6	4	0	2	6	5	8
Colombia	6	1	1	4	7	12	3
Venezuela	6	0	1	5	1	18	1

Group 12

Ecuador	0	Uruguay	2
Uruguay	1	Ecuador	0
Chile	0	Uruguay	0
Chile	4	Ecuador	1
Ecuador	1	Chile	1
Uruguay	2	Chile	0

	P	W	D	L	F	A	Pts
Uruguay	4	3	1	0	5	0	7
Chile	4	1	2	1	5	4	4
Ecuador	4	0	1	3	2	8	1

Group 13
Semi-finals:

Haiti	2	U.S.A.	0
U.S.A.	0	Haiti	1
Honduras	1	El Salvador	0
El Salvador	3	Honduras	0

Play-off in Mexico City:

El Salvador	3	Honduras	2

Final:

Haiti	1	El Salvador	2
El Salvador	0	Haiti	3

Play-off in Kingston:

El Salvador	1	Haiti	0

Group 14 MEXICO qualified as host country

Group 15

Sub-group A—staged in Seoul, South Korea

Australia	3	Japan	1
S. Korea	2	Japan	2
S. Korea	1	Australia	2
Japan	1	Australia	1
S. Korea	1	Australia	1
S. Korea	2	Japan	0

	P	W	D	L	F	A	Pts
Australia	4	2	2	0	7	4	6
S. Korea	4	1	2	1	6	5	4
Japan	4	0	2	2	4	8	2

Exceptional matches in Laurenco Marques:

Rhodesia	1	Australia	1
Rhodesia	0	Australia	0
Rhodesia	1	Australia	3

Sub-group B—played in Tel Aviv

Israel	4	New Zealand	0
Israel	2	New Zealand	0

Group Final:

Israel	1	Australia	0
Australia	1	Israel	1

Group 16

2nd Round matches:

Tunisia	0	Morocco	0
Morocco	0	Tunisia	0

Play-off in Marseilles:

Morocco	2	Tunisia	2

(Morocco qualified for final group matches on toss of a disc)

Ethiopia	1	Sudan	1
Sudan	3	Ethiopia	1

Nigeria	2	Ghana	1
Ghana	1	Nigeria	1

Final group:

Nigeria	2	Sudan	2
Morocco	2	Nigeria	1
Sudan	3	Nigeria	3
Sudan	0	Morocco	0
Morocco	3	Sudan	0
Nigeria	2	Morocco	0

	P	W	D	L	F	A	Pts
Morocco	4	2	1	1	5	3	5
Nigeria	4	1	2	1	8	7	4
Sudan	4	0	3	1	5	8	3

ENGLAND

	A	B	C	D	E	F	G	H	I	J
Banks	G	—	G	—	G	G	—	—	G	G
West	—	G	—	G	—	—	—	—	—	—
Bonetti	—	—	—	—	—	—	G	G	—	—
Newton	RB	RB	RB	RB¹	LB	LB	—	—	RB	—
Wright	—	—	—	RB²	RB	RB	RB	—	—	RB
Reaney	—	—	—	—	—	—	—	RB	—	—
McNab	LB	—	—	—	—	—	—	—	—	—
Cooper	—	LB	LB	LB	—	—	—	—	LB	LB
Hughes	—	—	—	—	—	—	LB	LB	—	LH
Mullery	RH	—	RH	RH	RH	RH	RH	RH	OR²	—
Labone	CH	—	CH	CH	CH	CH	—	—	—	CH
J. Charlton	—	CH	—	—	—	—	—	CH	CH	—
R. Moore	LH	RH	LH	LH	LH	LH	LH	LH	—	RH
Hunter	—	LH	—	—	—	—	—	—	LH	—
Ball	OR	OL	IR	IR	OR	OR	—	OL	—	IR
Lee	IR	OR	OR	OR	IL	—	OR¹	OR	OR¹	OR
Bell	—	IR	—	—	IR	IR	IR	IR¹	IR	—
R. Charlton	CF	IL	CF	CF	—	CF	CF	IL	IL	—
Astle	—	CF	—	—	—	—	—	CF	—	—
Thompson	—	—	—	—	—	—	OR²	—	—	—
Hurst	IL	—	IL	IL	CF	IL	IL	—	CF²	IL
Osgood	—	—	—	—	—	—	—	—	—	CF
Jones	—	—	—	—	—	—	—	—	CF¹	—
Peters	OL	—	OL	OL	OL	OL	OL	IR²	RH	OL
I. Storey-Moore	—	—	—	—	—	—	—	—	OL	—

WEST GERMANY (4-2-4 and *4-3-3)

A	26. 3. 69	W. Germany..............1 (G. Muller)	Wales..................1 (Barry Jones)	—	Frankfurt
B	16. 4. 69	Scotland.................1 (Murdoch)	W. Germany..............1 (G. Muller)	—	Glasgow
C	10. 5. 69	W. Germany..............1 (G. Muller)	Austria...................0	—	Mittelfeld
D	21. 5. 69	W. Germany..............12 (G. Muller 4, Overath 3, Haller 2, Lorenz, Held, Hottges)	Cyprus....................0	—	Essen
E	21. 9. 69	Austria...................1 (Pirkner)	W. Germany..............1 (G. Muller)	—	Vienna
F	24. 9. 69	Bulgaria..................0	W. Germany..............1 (Dorfel)	—	Sofia
G	22. 10. 69	W. Germany..............3 (Fichtel, G. Muller, Libuda)	Scotland..................2 (Johnstone, Gilzean)	—	Hamburg

	*A	*B	C	*D	E	F	*G
Maier	G	G¹	G	G	—	G	G
Wolter	—	G²	—	—	G	—	—
Vogts	RB	RB	LB	RB	LB	LB	LB
Schulz	RCB	RCB	LCB	RCB	LCB	RCB	RCB
Lorenz	LCB	LH²	—	LCB¹	—	—	—
Hottges	LH	—	RB	LB¹	RB	RB	RB
Patzke	LB	LCB	RCB	LCB²	—	—	—
Libuda	RH	—	—	RF	OR²	—	LF
Ulsass	CH¹	—	—	—	—	—	—
L. Muller	CH²	—	—	LB²	—	—	—
Gerd Muller	RF	CF	RCF	CF	LCF	LCF	CF
Held	CF	LF	LCF¹	LF	OL	—	—
Rebele	LF¹	—	—	—	—	—	—
B. Dorfel	LF²	RF	OR	—	OR¹	OR	—
Schnellinger	—	LB	—	—	—	—	—
Beckenbauer	—	RH	RH	CH	LH	RH	RH
Haller	—	CH	—	RH	—	—	CH
Overath	—	LH¹	LH	LH	RH	LH	LH
Heynckes	—	—	LCF²	—	—	—	—
Brenninger	—	—	OL¹	—	—	—	—
Volkert	—	—	OL²	—	—	—	—
Weber	—	—	—	—	RCB¹	—	—
Fichtel	—	—	—	—	RCB²	LCB	LCB
Uwe Seeler	—	—	—	—	RCF	RCF	RF
Maas	—	—	—	—	—	OL	—

BELGIUM (4-2-4 and *4-3-3)

A	16. 4. 69	Belgium...................2 (Puis, Van Himst)	Mexico...................0	—	Brussels
B	19. 10. 69	Yugoslavia...............4 (Belin, Dzajic, Spasovski 2)	Belgium...................0	—	Belgrade
C	5. 11. 69	Mexico...................1 (Onofre)	Belgium...................0	—	Mexico City
D	25. 2. 69	Belgium...................1 (Dockx)	England...................3 (Ball 2, Hurst)	—	Brussels

	A	*B	C	*D			A	*B	C	*D
Trappeniers	G	—	—	G		Hanon	—	RH	—	—
Piot	—	G	G	—		Semmeling	OR	—	—	RF
Heylens	RB	RB	RB	RB		Lambert	—	RF	—	—
Jeck	RCB	RCB	LCB	LCB		Verheyen	—	—	OR	LH²
Dewalque	LCB	—	RCB	RCB		Devrindt	RCF	—	—	CF
Beurlet	—	LCB	—	—		Van Himst	LCF	CF	—	LF
Thissen	LB	LB	LB	LB		Van Puymbroeck	—	—	LCF	—
Van Moer	RH	LH	RH	RH		Janssen	—	—	OL¹	—
Polleunis	LH	CH	RCF	LH¹		Depireux	—	—	OL²	—
Dockx	—	—	LH	CH		Puis	OL	LF	—	—

SWEDEN (4-2-4 and *4-3-3)

A	18. 2. 69	Israel .... 2 (Spiegel, Young)	Sweden .... 3 (Eiderstedt, Selander, Andersson)	—	Tel Aviv
B	26. 2. 69	Yugoslavia .... 2 (Bjekovic, Musemic)	Sweden .... 1 (Magnusson)	—	Belgrade
C	30. 4. 69	Sweden .... 1 (Kindvall)	Mexico 0	—	Malmo
D	22. 5. 69	Sweden .... 4 (Johansson 2, Svensson, Kautonen o.g.)	Finland 0	—	Vaxjo
E	1. 6. 69	Sweden .... 4 (Eiderstedt 2, Palsson, Andersson)	Norway .... 2 (Iversen, Berg)	—	Gothenburg
F	19. 6. 69	Norway .... 2 (Dyb.Olsen 2)	Sweden .... 5 (Persson, Eriksson, Kindvall, Grahn, Grip)	—	Oslo
G	25. 6. 69	Denmark.................. 0	Sweden .... 1 (Eklund)	—	Copenhagen
H	6. 8. 69	U.S.S.R. 0	Sweden .... 1 (Eklund)	—	Moscow
I	24. 9. 69	Sweden .... 2 (Nicklasson, Grahn)	Hungary 0	—	Stockholm
J	15. 10. 69	Sweden .... 2 (Kindvall 2)	France.................... 0	—	Stockholm
K	1. 11. 69	France.................... 3 (Bras 2, Djorkaeff)	Sweden 0	—	Paris

	*A	B	C	D	*E	*F	*G	H	*I	*J	K
R. Hellstrom	G	G	—	—	—	—	—	—	G¹	G	G
S-G. Larsson	—	—	G	—	—	—	G	—	G²	—	—
R. Pettersson	—	—	—	G	G	G	—	G	—	—	—
Selander	RB	RB	RB	RB	RB	RB	RB	RB	RB	RB	LB
Grip	LB	LB	—	—	LB	LB	LB	LB	LB	LB	LB
Karlsson	—	—	LB	—	—	—	—	—	—	—	—
Nordqvist	LCB	LCB	LCB	LCB	LCB	LCB	LCB	LCB	LCB¹	LCB	LCB
K. Kristensson	RCB	RCB	RCB	RCB	—	—	RCB	RCB	LCB²	—	RCB
Axelsson	—	—	—	LB	RCB	RCB	—	—	RCB	RCB	—
Tommy Svensson	RH¹	RH	RH	RH	RH	CH	CH	RH	RH	RH	RH¹
Leif Eriksson	LH	LH	OR	OR	LH	RH	RH	RCF¹	RF	CH¹	RB
Jan Olsson	CH	—	—	LH	CH	LF²	CH	—	—	—	—
Eiderstedt	RF	OL¹	RCF	—	CF	—	RF	—	—	—	—
Rolf Andersson	CF	OL²	—	—	LF	—	—	—	—	—	—
Ljungbert	RH²	—	—	—	—	—	—	—	—	—	—
Christiansson	LF	—	—	OL	—	—	—	—	—	—	—
Magnusson	—	OR	—	—	—	—	—	—	—	CH²	OR
Sten Palsson	—	—	—	—	RF	—	LF	OL	—	—	—
Ove Grahn	—	RCF	—	LCF	—	RF	—	—	CF	RF	RCF
Sven Lindman	—	—	—	—	—	—	—	OR	—	—	—
Johansson	—	—	OL	RCF	—	—	—	—	LF	—	OL¹
Thos Nordahl	—	LCF	—	—	—	—	—	—	—	—	—
Ove Kindvall	—	—	LCF	—	—	CF	—	—	—	CF	—
Eklund	—	—	—	—	—	—	CF	LCF	—	—	OL²
Orjan Persson	—	—	—	—	—	LF¹	—	—	—	LF	—
Turesson	—	—	—	—	—	—	—	—	—	—	LCF
Sandberg	—	—	—	—	—	—	—	RCF²	—	—	—
Bo Larsson	—	—	LH	—	—	LH	—	LH	LH	LH	LH
Nicklasson	—	—	—	—	—	—	—	—	CH	—	RH²

BULGARIA (4-2-4 and *4-3-3)

A	23. 4. 69	Bulgaria .... 2 (Asparoukov 2)	Luxembourg .... 1 (Leonard)	—	Sofia
B	22. 5. 69	Italy...................... 0	Bulgaria 0	—	Turin
C	15. 6. 69	Bulgaria .... 4 (Bonev, Asparoukov, Penev, Dermendiev)	Poland.................... 1 (Deyna)	—	Sofia
D	24. 9. 69	Bulgaria 0	W. Germany.............. 1 (B. Dorfel)	—	Sofia
E	22. 10. 69	Netherlands .... 1 (Veenstra)	Bulgaria .... 1 (Bonev)	—	Rotterdam
F	9. 11. 69	Poland.................... 3 (Jarosik 2, Deyna)	Bulgaria 0	—	Warsaw
G	7. 12. 69	Luxembourg.............. 1 (Philippe)	Bulgaria .... 3 (Leszczynski, Yakimov, Bonev)	—	Luxembourg
H	28. 12. 69	Morocco .... 3 (Maaroufi 2, Ghazouani)	Bulgaria 0	—	Casablanca

	A	B	*C	D	*E	*F	G	H
Simeonov	G	G	G	G	G	G¹	G	G
Aladjov	RB	RB	—	—	LCB	LB	—	—
Pechev.............	—	—	RB	—	—	—	—	—
Chalamanov.......	—	—	—	RB	RB	RB	RB	—
Gaidarski	—	—	—	—	—	—	—	RB
Penev.............	RCB	RCB	LCB	LH	RH	RH	LH	RCB
Gaganelov........	LCB	LCB	RCB	LCB	—	—	LB	LB
Ivkov.............	—	LB	LB	RCB	—	—	—	—
Dimitrov..........	—	—	—	—	RCB	RCB	RCB	LCB²
Jetchev	LB	RH	RH	—	LB	LCB	LCB	LCB¹
Davidov	—	—	—	LB	—	—	—	—
Bonev	RH	LH	CH	LCF	CH	CH	RCF	RH
Yakimov	LH	—	—	RH¹	RF²	—	RH	LCF¹
Popov	OR¹	—	—	—	—	—	—	—
Dermendiev	OL	OR	RF	OR	RF¹	RF	OR	OR
Jekov............	OR²	—	—	RH²	—	CF	OL	—
Asparoukov.......	RCF	RCF	CF	RCF	CF	—	LCF	RCF
Mitkov	LCF	—	—	OL²	—	—	—	—
T. Kolev	—	LCF	LH	LH	—	LH	LH	LCF²
Kotzev...........	—	OL	LF	OL¹	—	—	—	—
Philippov	—	—	—	—	—	G²	—	—
Gheorghiev........	—	—	—	—	LF¹	—	—	OL
Mikhailov	—	—	—	—	LF²	LF²	—	—
Maraszliev	—	—	—	—	—	LF¹	—	—
Nikodimov	—	—	—	—	—	—	—	LH

ITALY (4-2-4 and *4-3-3)

A	29. 3. 69	E. Germany .... 2 (Vogel, Kreisch)	Italy...................... 2 (Riva 2)	—	E. Berlin
B	22. 5. 69	Italy...................... 0	Bulgaria 0	—	Turin
C	4. 11. 69	Italy...................... 4 (Riva 3, Mazzola)	Wales..................... 1 (England)	—	Rome
D	22. 11. 69	Italy...................... 3 (Mazzola, Domenghini, Riva)	E. Germany 0	—	Naples

	*A	B	*C	D		*A	B	*C	D
Zoff	G	G	—	G	De Sisti	CH	LH	CH	LH
Albertosi	—	—	G	—	Rivera	LH	—	LH	—
Burgnich	RB	RB¹	RB	RB	Cera............	—	—	—	RH¹
Poletti	—	RB²	—	—	Prati	RF	—	—	—
Castano........	RCB	—	—	—	Domenghini	—	OR	RF	LCF
Puia............	—	RCB	RCB	RCB	Chiaruggi	—	—	—	OR
Salvadore	LCB	LCB	LCB	LCB	Mazzola	CF	RCF	CF²	RCF
Facchetti.......	LB	LB	LB	LB	Riva............	LF	OL	LF	OL
Bertini	RH	RH	RH¹	—	Anastasi.........	—	LCF	CF¹	—
Juliano	—	—	RH²	RH²					

PERU

A 6. 4. 69 Brazil 2 (Jairzinho, Gerson) — Peru 1 (Gallardo) — Rio
B 9. 4. 69 Brazil 3 (Pelé, Tostão, Edu) — Peru 2 (Gallardo, Baylon) — Rio
C 9. 5. 69 Colombia 1 (Gonzales) — Peru 3 (Ramirez, Cubilla, Leon) — Bogota
D 20. 5. 69 Mexico 0 — Peru 1 (Leon) — Mexico City
E 25. 5. 69 Mexico 3 (Borja 2, Bustos) — Peru 0 — Mexico City
F 19. 6. 69 Peru 1 (Chumpitaz) — Colombia 1 (Gallego) — Lima
G 28. 6. 69 Peru 1 (Leon) — Uruguay 0 — Lima
H 10. 7. 69 Peru 2 (Cubilla 2) — Paraguay 1 (Mora) — Lima
I 19. 7. 69 Peru 2 (Leon 2) — Paraguay 1 (Sosa) — Lima
J 3. 8. 69 Peru 1 (Leon) — Argentina 0 — Lima
K 10. 8. 69 Bolivia 2 (Alvarez, Chumpitaz o.g.) — Peru 1 (Challe) — La Paz
L 18. 8. 69 Peru 3 (Cubilla, Challe, Gallardo) — Bolivia 0 — Lima
M 31. 8. 69 Argentina 2 (Albrecht, Rendo) — Peru 2 (Ramirez 2) — Buenos Aires

	A	B	C	D	E	F	G	H	I	J	K	L	M
Sartor	G	G	G	—	G	—	—	—	—	—	—	—	—
Rubinos	—	—	—	G	—	G	G	G¹	G	G	G	G	G
Correa	—	—	—	—	—	G²	—	—	—	—	—	—	—
J. Gonzalez	RB	RB	—	RB	RB	RB	—	—	—	—	—	—	RB
Campos	—	—	RB	RB	—	—	—	—	RB²	—	—	—	RB
P. Gonzalez	LB	LB	LB	—	—	—	—	RB	RB¹	RB	RB¹	RB	—
Elias	—	—	—	LB	—	—	—	—	—	—	—	—	—
Fuentes	—	—	—	—	—	LB	LB	LB	LB	LB	LB	—	—
Risco	—	—	—	—	—	—	—	—	—	—	—	LB	LB
Mifflin	RH	RH	RH	RH	RH	IR	RH	RH	IR	RH	RH	—	—
La Torre	CH	CH¹	CH	CH	CH	CH	CH	—	—	CH	CH	CH	CH
J. Fernandez	—	CH²	—	—	—	—	—	CH	CH	RB²	—	—	—
Chumpitaz	LH	LH	LH	LH	LB	LH	LH	LH	LH	LH	LH	LH	LH
Baylon	OR¹	IR	—	OR	OR	OR	OR	OR	OR	OR	OR	OR	OR
Munante	OR²	—	IL	—	OL²	—	—	—	—	—	—	—	—
Casaretto	—	OR¹	OR¹	OL	IL	—	—	—	—	—	—	—	—
Barreto	—	OR²	—	—	—	—	—	—	—	—	—	—	—
Cubilla	IR	IL	IR	IL	IR	IL	IL	CF	IL	IL	IL	IL	IL
Challe	IL²	—	OR²	IR	LH	RH	IR	IR	RH	IR	IR	RH	RH
Cruzado	—	—	—	—	—	—	—	—	—	—	—	IR	IR
Leon	CF	CF	CF	CF	CF	CF	CF	—	CF	CF	CF	CF	CF
V. Zegarra	IL¹	—	—	—	—	—	—	—	—	—	—	—	—
Rojas	—	—	—	—	—	—	—	IL	—	—	—	—	—
Gallardo	OL	OL	—	—	—	OL	OL	OL	OL	OL	OL	OL¹	—
Ramirez	—	—	OL	—	OL¹	—	—	—	—	—	—	—	OL
A. Zegarra	—	—	—	—	—	—	—	—	—	—	—	OL²	—

SOVIET UNION (4-2-4 and *4-3-3)

A	21. 2. 69	Colombia ... 1 (Santa)	U.S.S.R. ... 3 (Gershkovich, Khmelnitsky 2)	—	Bogota
B	26. 7. 69	E. Germany ... 2 (Lowe, Frenzel)	U.S.S.R. ... 2 (Puzach, Khmelnitsky)	—	Leipzig
C	6. 8. 69	U.S.S.R. ... 0	Sweden ... 1 (Eklund)	—	Moscow
D	10. 9. 69	N. Ireland ... 0	U.S.S.R. ... 0	—	Belfast
E	24. 9. 69	Yugoslavia ... 1 (Dzajic)	U.S.S.R. ... 3 (Asatiani, Nodia, Bishovets)	—	Belgrade
F	15. 10. 69	U.S.S.R. ... 3 (Muntyan 2, Nodia)	Turkey ... 0	—	Kiev
G	22. 10. 69	U.S.S.R. ... 2 (Nodia, Bishovets)	N. Ireland ... 0	—	Moscow
H	16. 11. 69	Turkey ... 1 (Ender)	U.S.S.R. ... 3 (Asatiani 2, Khmelnitsky)	—	Istanbul

	*A	*B	C	*D	E	F	G	H
Psenitchnikov	G	—	—	—	—	—	—	—
Ponomarev	RB	LCB	RB	—	—	—	—	—
Dzodziashvili	LB	—	—	RCB	RB	RB	RB	RB
Chesternev	RCB	RCB	RCB	LCB	LCB	LCB	LCB	LCB
Kaplicznij	LCB	RB	LCB	LB	LB	LB	LB	—
Jeskov	RH	CH	—	—	—	—	—	—
Gershkovich	CH	—	—	—	—	RCF	RCF[1]	—
Muntyan	LH	RH	—	CH	LH	LH	LH	LH
Khmelnitsky	RF	CF	OL	LF[1]	—	—	—	LCF
Lissenko	CF	—	—	—	—	—	—	—
Chumakov	LF	—	OR[1]	—	—	—	—	—
Rudakov	—	G	G	G	G	G	G	—
Kavazashvili	—	—	—	—	—	—	—	G
Lovtchev	—	LB	LB	LH	RCB	RCB	RCB	LB
Khurtsilava	—	LH[1]	—	—	—	—	—	RCB
Kiselev	—	LH[2]	RH	RH	—	—	—	—
Serebriankov	—	—	—	—	RH	RH	RH	RH
Osianine	—	—	LH	—	RCF	—	—	—
Puzach	—	RF	LCF	CF	—	—	RCF[2]	—
Husainov	—	LF[1]	RCF[1]	RF	—	—	—	—
Asatiani	—	—	—	—	OR	OR	OR	OR
Papaev	—	—	OR[2]	—	—	—	—	—
Bishovets	—	—	—	—	LCF	LCF	LCF	RCF
Nodia	—	—	—	—	OL	OL	OL	OL
Metreveli	—	LF[2]	RCF[2]	—	—	—	—	—
Evrnjikhin	—	—	—	LF[2]	—	—	—	—
Afonin	—	—	—	RB	—	—	—	—

BRAZIL (4-2-4 and *4-3-3)

A	6. 4. 69	Brazil (Jairzinho, Gerson)	2	Peru (Gallardo)	1	— Rio
B	9. 4. 69	Brazil (Pelé, Tostão, Edu)	3	Peru (Gallardo, Baylon)	2	— Rio
C	12. 6. 69	Brazil (Tostão, Jairzinho)	2	England (Bell)	1	— Rio
D	7. 8. 69	Colombia	0	Brazil (Tostão 2)	2	— Bogota
E	10. 8. 69	Venezuela	0	Brazil (Tostão 3, Pelé 2)	5	— Caracas
F	18. 8. 69	Paraguay	0	Brazil (Edu 2, Jairzinho)	3	— Asuncion
G	21. 8. 69	Brazil (Pelé, Tostão 2, Edu, Jairzinho, Rivelino)	6	Colombia (Gallego 2)	2	— Rio
H	24. 8. 69	Brazil (Tostão 3, Pelé 2, Jairzinho)	6	Venezuela	0	— Rio
I	31. 8. 69	Brazil (Pelé)	1	Paraguay	0	— Rio

	*A	*B	C	D	E	F	G	H	I
Felix	G	G	—	G	G	G	G	G¹	G
Gylmar	—	—	G	—	—	—	—	—	—
Lula	—	—	—	—	—	—	—	G²	—
Carlos Alberto	RB	RB	RB	RB	RB	RB	RB	RB	RB
Brito	RCB	RCB	—	—	—	—	—	LCB²	—
Djalma Dias	LCB	LCB	RCB	RCB	RCB	RCB	RCB	RCB	RCB
Joel	—	CH²	LCB	LCB	LCB	LCB	LCB	LCB¹	LCB
Rildo	LB	LB	LB	LB	LB	LB	LB	LB	LB
Dirceu Lopes	RH	RH¹	—	—	—	—	—	—	—
Piazza	CH	CH¹	—	RH	RH	RH	RH	RH	RH
Gerson	LH	LH	LH	LH	LH	LH	LH¹	LH	LH
Rivelino	—	—	—	—	—	—	LH²	—	—
Jairzinho	RF	RF	OR	OR	OR	OR	OR	OR	OR
Tostão	LF	LF¹	RCF	RCF	RCF	RCF	RCF	RCF	RCF
Pelé	CF¹	CF	LCF	LCF	LCF	LCF	LCF¹	LCF	LCF
Edu	CF²	RH²	OL¹	OL	OL	OL	OL	OL	OL
Clodoaldo	—	—	RH	—	—	—	—	—	—
Cesar	—	LF²	OL²	—	—	—	LCF²	—	—

RUMANIA (4-2-4)

A	15. 1. 69	England (J. Charlton)	1	Rumania (Dumitrache)	1	— Wembley
B	16. 4. 69	Greece (Sideris, Dedes)	2	Rumania (Dumitrache 2)	2	— Athens
C	14. 5. 69	Switzerland	0	Rumania (Michaud o.g.)	1	— Lausanne
D	3. 9. 69	Yugoslavia (Mujkic)	1	Rumania (Dembrovski)	1	— Belgrade
E	8. 10. 69	Rumania (Dobrin)	1	Portugal	0	— Bucharest
F	16. 11. 69	Rumania (Dembrovski)	1	Greece (Domazos)	1	— Bucharest

	A	B	C	D	E	F
Gornea	G	—	—	—	—	—
Raducanu	—	G	G	—	G	G
Gice	—	—	—	G	—	—
Satmareanu	RB	RB	RB¹	RB	RB	RB
Boc	RCB	LCB	RCB	—	—	—
Dan Coe	—	RCB	LCB	LB	LCB	LCB
Halmageanu	—	—	RB²	RCB	RCB	RCB
Dinu	LCB	RH	RH	RH	RH	RH
Mocanu	—	—	—	LCB	—	—
Deleanu	LB	LB	LB	—	LB	LB
Anca	RH	—	—	—	—	—

	A	B	C	D	E	F
Radu Nunweiler	LH	—	LH	—	LH	LH
Ghergheli	—	LH	—	LH	—	—
Dembrovski	OR	OR	OR	OR	OR	OR
Domide	RCF	—	—	LCF	—	—
Ionescu	—	RCF	—	—	—	—
Dumitrache	LCF	LCF	RCF	RCF	LCF	LCF
Dobrin	—	—	—	—	RCF	RCF
Tufan	—	—	LCF	—	—	—
Lucescu	OL	OL	OL	—	OL	OL
Creiniceanu	—	—	—	OL	—	—

URUGUAY (4-3-3)

A	8. 6. 69	Uruguay .... 1 (Cubilla)	England .... 2 (Lee, Hurst)	—	Montevideo	
B	28. 6. 69	Peru .... 1 (Leon)	Uruguay 0	—	Lima	
C	3. 7. 69	Colombia 0	Uruguay .... 1 (Bareno)	—	Bogota	
D	6. 7. 69	Ecuador 0	Uruguay .... 2 (Bareno, Zubia)	—	Guayaquil	
E	13. 7. 69	Chile 0	Uruguay 0	—	Santiago	
F	20. 7. 69	Uruguay .... 1 (Anchetta)	Ecuador 0	—	Montevideo	
G	10. 8. 69	Uruguay .... 2 (Cortes, Rocha)	Chile 0	—	Montevideo	

	A	B	C	D	E	F	G
Maidana	G	—	—	—	—	—	—
Mazurkiewicz	—	G	G	G	G	G	G
Ubinas	RB	RB	RB	RB	RB	RB	RB
Anchetta	RCB	RCB	RCB	RCB	RCB	RCB	RCB
Paz	LCB	—	—	—	—	—	—
Matosas	LH	LCB	LCB	LCB	LCB	LCB	LCB
Mujica	LB	LB²	—	—	—	—	—
Caetano	—	LB	LB¹	LB	LB	LB	LB
Montero-Castillo	RH	RH	RH	RH	RH	RH	RH
Julio C. Cortes	CH	CH	CH¹	CH	CH	CH	CH
Rocha	—	LH	LH	LH	LH¹	—	LH
Cubilla	RF	RF	RF¹	RF	RF	LH	RF
Sergio Silva	—	—	—	—	—	RF	CF¹
Hector Silva	CF	CF	CF	CF¹	—	CF	—
Acuna	—	—	—	—	—	—	CF²
Zubia	—	—	RF²	CF²	CF	—	—
Morales	LF	—	—	—	—	—	—
Techera	—	—	CH²	—	—	—	—
Forte	—	—	—	—	LH²	—	—
Bareno	—	LF	LF	LF	LF	LF	LF

CZECHOSLOVAKIA (4-2-4 and *4-3-3)

A	16. 4. 69	Netherlands .... 2 (Roggeven 2)	Czechoslovakia 0	—	Rotterdam
B	3. 5. 69	Rep. of Ireland .... 1 (Rogers)	Czechoslovakia .... 2 (Kabat, Adamec)	—	Dublin
C	25. 5. 69	Hungary .... 2 (A. Dunai, Albert)	Czechoslovakia 0	—	Budapest
D	14. 9. 69	Czechoslovakia .... 3 (Hagara, Kuna, Kvasnak)	Hungary .... 3 (Bene, A. Dunai, Fazekas)	—	Prague
E	8. 10. 69	Czechoslovakia .... 3 (Adamec 3)	Rep. of Ireland 0	—	Prague
F	3. 12. 69	Czechoslovakia .... 4 (Kvasnak, Fr. Vesely, Adamec, Jokl)	Hungary .... 1 (Kocsics)	—	*Marseilles*

	A	B	C	*D	E	F
Vencel	G	G	G	—	—	G²
Viktor	—	—	—	G	G	G¹
Dobias	RB	RB	RB¹	—	—	—
Pivarnik	—	—	RB²	RB	RB	RB
Plass	RCB	RCB	RCB	RCB¹	—	—
Migas	—	—	—	—	RCB¹	RCB
Horvath	LCB	LCB	LCB	LCB	LCB	LCB
Hagara	LB	LB	—	LB	LB	LB
Ziocha	—	—	LB	—	—	—
Geleta	RH	—	—	—	—	—
Szikora	LCF²	RH¹	RH	RH¹	—	—
Hrdlicka	LH²	RH²	—	—	—	—

	A	B	C	*D	E	F
Pollak	—	—	—	RH²	—	LH²
Kuna	LH¹	—	LH	LH	LH	LH¹
Kvasnak	—	LH	—	CH	RH	RH
B. Vesely	OR	OR	OR	RF	OR	—
Fr. Vesely	—	—	—	—	—	OR
Jokl	RCF	—	RCF	—	RCF²	OL
Jurkanin	—	RCF	—	—	RCF¹	—
Petras	—	—	—	—	—	RCF
Adamec	LCF¹	LCF	LCF	CF	LCF	LCF
Kabat	OL	OL	OL	—	OL	—
Jan Capkovic	—	—	—	—	LF	—
Hrivnak	—	—	—	—	RCB²	RCB²

WORLD CUP 1970

Group I (Mexico City)
Mexico	0	U.S.S.R.	0
Belgium	3	El Salvador	0
U.S.S.R.	4	Belgium	1
Mexico	4	El Salvador	0
El Salvador	0	U.S.S.R.	2
Mexico	1	Belgium	0

Group Winners: U.S.S.R
Runners-up: MEXICO

Group II (Fuebla)
Uruguay	2	Israel	0
Uruguay	0	Italy	0
Sweden	1	Uruguay	0

Group II (Toluca)
Italy	1	Sweden	0
Sweden	1	Israel	1
Italy	0	Israel	0

Group Winners: ITALY
Runners-up: URUGUAY

Group III (Guadalajara)
Rumania	0	England	1
Czechoslovakia	1	Brazil	4
Rumania	2	Czechoslovakia	1
Brazil	1	England	0
Brazil	3	Rumania	2
Czechoslovakia	0	England	1

Group Winners: BRAZIL
Runners-up: ENGLAND

Group IV (Leon)
Peru	3	Bulgaria	2
Morocco	1	W. Germany	2
Peru	3	Morocco	0
W. Germany	5	Bulgaria	2
W. Germany	3	Peru	1
Morocco	1	Bulgaria	1

Group Winners: W. GERMANY
Runners-up: PERU

Quarter-Finals

Match A (Mexico City)

U.S.S.R. 0 - 1 URUGUAY
(Gr. I Winner) A.E.T. (Gr. II Runner-up)

Match B (Toluca)

ITALY 4 - 1 MEXICO
Gr. II Winner) (Gr. I Runner-up)

Match C (Guadalajara)

BRAZIL 4 - 2 PERU
(Gr. III Winner) (Gr. IV Runner-up)

Match D (Leon)

W. GERMANY 3 - 2 ENGLAND
(Gr. IV Winner) A.E.T. (Gr. III Runner-up)

Semi-Finals

URUGUAY 1 - 3 BRAZIL
(Winner Match A) (Winner Match C)

ITALY 4 - 3 W. GERMANY
(Winner Match B) A.E.T. (Winner Match D)

Match to decide 3rd and 4th ratings
(between beaten semi-finalists)

URUGUAY 0 - 1 W. GERMANY

FINAL

BRAZIL 4 - 1 ITALY